Eco-Label Visual Design and Sustainability

Carmela Donato

Eco-Label Visual Design and Sustainability

The Impact on Consumer Perceptions
and Market Trends

Carmela Donato
Department of Economics
University of Roma Tre
Rome, Italy

ISBN 978-3-031-82760-0   ISBN 978-3-031-82761-7   (eBook)
https://doi.org/10.1007/978-3-031-82761-7

Cover illustration: © Melisa Hasan

This Palgrave Macmillan imprint is published by the registered company Springer Nature Switzerland AG
The registered company address is: Gewerbestrasse 11, 6330 Cham, Switzerland

If disposing of this product, please recycle the paper.

FOREWORD

Research is most valuable when it combines methodological precision with passion, and this book is a testament to that synergy. Carmela Donato is a scholar whose work reflects both intellectual rigor and a deep commitment to sustainability. Her research has explored sustainability from multiple perspectives, including fashion, food packaging, food consumption, and aesthetics. This book focuses on a singular yet impactful element: eco-label certifications and their role in visually and aesthetically communicating sustainability.

Through a multidisciplinary lens (aesthetic, psychology, and consumer behavior), it highlights the significance of visual and conceptual complexity, color schemes, and textual clarity in shaping attitudes toward sustainability. With empirical rigor, the author provides insights that extend beyond theory, offering practical guidelines for designers, regulators, and businesses aiming to strengthen sustainable branding efforts.

Eco-labels are not merely certifications; they are fundamental tools for sustainability communication and green marketing. Through a nuanced analysis of design elements, this book reveals how visual choices influence sustainability perceptions. As sustainability becomes a priority across industries, eco-labels serve as key instruments in guiding consumers toward responsible choices. However, their impact is often diminished by consumer confusion and inconsistent visual communication. This book addresses these challenges directly, presenting an extensive empirical study on how eco-label design influences perceptions of sustainability and consumer behavior.

From a theoretical perspective, this book systematically examines how design elements shape consumer perceptions, contributing to the growing discourse on sustainable consumption and visual communication. It presents a well-structured and compelling argument for why eco-labels should be seen not merely as promotional tools but as catalysts for change.

Carmela Donato's ability to bridge academic research and practical applications makes this book a valuable resource for a broad audience. It is a rigorous contribution to the study of sustainable consumption while also offering actionable insights for businesses seeking to enhance green marketing strategies and policymakers working to refine eco-label regulations.

Her commitment to sustainability research is driven by the belief that knowledge should serve a greater purpose—helping build a more responsible and environmentally conscious world. This work is an invitation to rethink how we communicate sustainability, making it more accessible, comprehensible, and ultimately more effective in shaping consumer behavior toward responsible choices.

It is rare to find a researcher who not only masters the complexities of her field but also conveys them with clarity and purpose. Carmela Donato does precisely this, and I am certain that her work will spark further dialogue and inspire meaningful change.

Simona Romani
Luiss University
Rome, Italy

CONTENTS

LIST OF FIGURES

LIST OF TABLES

CHAPTER 1

Introduction

Abstract This book examines the pivotal role of eco-labels in promoting
sustainability, exploring how their visual design influences consumer
perceptions and behaviors. While eco-labels serve as signals of environmental and ethical responsibility, their effectiveness hinges on aesthetic
elements like complexity, color, and text. Grounded in marketing, design,
and consumer psychology, the book integrates Berlyne's aesthetic theories with empirical findings, demonstrating how well-designed eco-labels
enhance trust, familiarity, and sustainability perceptions. Through case
studies and an original study using real eco-labels, it provides practical insights for marketers, designers, and policymakers to create visually
engaging labels that foster sustainable consumer behavior.

Keywords Eco-Labels · Sustainability · Aesthetic Psychology ·
Consumer Perceptions · Visual Design

In today's consumer-driven marketplace, sustainability has evolved from a
niche concern into a widespread expectation, shaping both purchasing
decisions and brand positioning. To meet this growing demand, eco-
labels have become essential tools for companies. These labels indicate
that a product is sustainably produced, signaling environmental and
ethical responsibility. In doing so, they enhance perceptions of both

the product and the brand, appealing not only to socially responsible consumers but also to those less focused on sustainability.

Despite the presence of more than 400 eco-labels across 199 countries and 25 industries,[1] along with a steady increase in eco-labeled products since September 2023,[2] consumer understanding and familiarity with these labels remain limited. This is consistent with Statista (2023)[3] data, which shows that 50% of surveyed UK consumers reported not adopting a more sustainable lifestyle in the past 12 months due to a lack of information.

For eco-labels to be truly effective, they must do more than inform; they must engage consumers visually. Design plays a critical role in capturing attention, building trust, and conveying sustainability in a way that aligns with consumer values.

This book analyzes the complex relationship between the visual design elements of eco-labels and consumer perceptions, focusing on how design can more effectively communicate sustainability. Grounded in research from marketing, design, and consumer psychology, it explores the intricate relationship between visual design elements and consumer perceptions of eco-labels, illustrating how these elements convey sustainability to consumers.

The core of the book comprises a comprehensive review of existing literature on eco-labels, emphasizing the pivotal role of visual design in shaping consumer behavior. This includes an examination of the impact of visual aesthetics on consumer behavior, specifically focusing on the literature surrounding logo design and its influence on evaluations. Additionally, findings from an empirical study are presented, which considers real eco-labels and assesses their efficacy in influencing consumer perceptions of sustainability and adoption through visual design.

In particular, Chapter 2 underscores how eco-labels serve as crucial signals in a marketplace increasingly driven by consumers' desire for sustainable products. It distinguishes between the different types of eco-labels and the various stakeholders involved in their effectiveness. Moreover, the chapter includes several case studies illustrating how leading

---

[1] https://www.ecolabelindex.com/

[2] https://environment.ec.europa.eu/topics/circular-economy/eu-ecolabel/business/ecolabel-facts-and-figures_en

[3] https://www.statista.com/statistics/1325237/why-consumers-have-not-adopted-a-more-sustainable-lifestyle-uk/

brands leverage certification to drive consumer preference and achieve market success. Finally, it discusses consumers' perceptions of eco-labels, highlighting the challenges related to familiarity, trust, and understanding of these certifications.

While eco-labels provide essential information about sustainability, aesthetics are equally important in shaping consumer interpretation and response. Chapter 3 highlights the strong link between aesthetic psychology and consumer behavior, demonstrating how the visual appeal of products, packaging, and branding significantly affects preferences. Grounded in the work of Daniel E. Berlyne, a pioneer in Aesthetic Psychology, the chapter analyzes key aesthetic variables (i.e., psychophysical and collative) that influence aesthetic appreciation.

Incorporating these principles into eco-label design is crucial for brands aiming to effectively communicate sustainability. Berlyne's theories suggest that designs balancing complexity and visual appeal can enhance consumer engagement with both the label and the product. Since consumers often rely on visual cues for quick judgments, the design of an eco-label logo can play a pivotal role in addressing challenges related to eco-label perceptions, particularly familiarity, trust, and understanding of the sustainable meaning behind these certifications.

In addition to reviewing existing literature on eco-label effectiveness and aesthetics in consumer research, Chapter 3 presents an original empirical study evaluating the effectiveness of real-world eco-labels based on their visual design and resulting impact. Specifically, the study examines how key design factors—such as visual and conceptual complexity, color, and the amount of text—affect consumer perceptions of sustainability and the adoption of eco-labels. By using actual eco-labels as visual stimuli, the study offers practical, evidence-based insights for improving eco-label design, ultimately enhancing their effectiveness in promoting sustainable consumer behavior.

The concluding chapter synthesizes insights from previous sections, emphasizing the research's contributions to consumer behavior and sustainable marketing. It discusses the practical implications for businesses and policymakers while suggesting avenues for future research.

In conclusion, this book connects theory and practice by illustrating how design choices in eco-labels influence consumer perceptions and behaviors. It offers practical guidance for marketers and designers on creating informative and visually appealing eco-labels that can build consumer trust and promote sustainable practices. Policymakers will also find valuable insights on how eco-label design can encourage more sustainable consumer behaviors.

Additionally, by integrating theoretical insights from scholars with empirical evidence, the book equips businesses, designers, policymakers, and researchers in marketing, consumer behavior, sustainable development, and environmental studies with the tools needed to communicate sustainability effectively through visual design.

CHAPTER 2

Eco-Label as a Sustainable Communication Tool

Abstract This chapter examines eco-labels as key tools for green communication, helping consumers align purchasing decisions with sustainability. It provides an overview of eco-label types and the regulations ensuring their credibility, while analyzing the roles of key stakeholders—consumers, producers, and third-party organizations. Through case studies, the chapter highlights the successful brand adoption of eco-labels, showcasing their integration into marketing strategies to promote sustainability and build trust. Moreover, it addresses the barriers to broader adoption, focusing on challenges such as low consumer awareness and limited understanding of the sustainability messages eco-labels convey.

Keywords Eco-Labels · Green communication · Sustainability · Stakeholders · Business cases

1 INTRODUCTION

In a time of growing environmental awareness and the demand for sustainable practices, eco-label logos play a crucial role in helping consumers align their purchasing decisions with their values. They raise awareness about environmental issues, provide information on product sustainability, and foster trust and responsibility in the marketplace.

C. Donato, *Eco-Label Visual Design and Sustainability*,
https://doi.org/10.1007/978-3-031-82761-7_2

This chapter offers a deeper understanding of how eco-label logos function as essential components in the broader narrative of sustainability, equipping consumers and marketers with the knowledge they need to make informed choices in an increasingly complex marketplace. It examines the various roles eco-labels play in sustainable communication, highlighting how they guide consumers toward environmentally friendly products.

A comprehensive overview of the different types of eco-labels is provided, detailing the criteria and standards they represent, with an emphasis on the regulations that ensure their credibility and the key actors involved in these processes. Additionally, case studies and real-world examples of successful initiatives illustrate the effectiveness of eco-labels in promoting sustainable options.

In particular, the first section explores how eco-labels serve as signals, helping consumers navigate a crowded marketplace and reinforcing sustainable choices through effective marketing strategies. The second section provides an in-depth examination of various types of eco-labels, discussing their specific criteria and standards.

The third section highlights the key players in the eco-label ecosystem and their roles in ensuring the success of these initiatives, followed by an analysis of how leading brands leverage eco-labels to enhance their market presence and foster sustainable consumptions. Finally, the chapter concludes by examining the role of eco-labels in influencing consumer behavior and promoting sustainability across various sectors. It also addresses the challenges, benefits, and socio-demographic factors that affect eco-label perception, along with the growing concerns about greenwashing that threaten their credibility.

2   Green Marketing: Driving Sustainable Choices Through Signals: The Role of Eco-Labels

Marketing strategies act as a driving force in the production processes of both products and services; indeed, they provide crucial insights that shape the product concept and guide its design, ensuring that what is created aligns with consumer needs and market demands (Dangelico & Vocalelli, 2017). In today's world, marketing plays a crucial role in addressing environmental challenges, giving rise to concepts such as ecological, environmental, and green marketing. These strategies are key to promoting sustainable practices and raising awareness about environmental responsibility (Papadas et al., 2017). The term *Green Marketing* developed between the late 1970s and early 1990s. The first definition of Green Marketing dates back to 1976, and it was defined as a concept that "*concerns all marketing activities that serve to prevent environmental problems and that can provide a remedy to environmental problems*" (Dangelico & Vocalelli, 2017). Over the years, many definitions have been provided, and the concept has evolved to become more structured, as seen in the definition of Sustainable Marketing as "*the process of planning, implementing, and controlling the development, pricing, promotion, and distribution of products in a way that meets the following three criteria: (1) customer needs are satisfied, (2) organizational goals are achieved, and (3) the process is compatible with ecosystem themes*" (Dangelico & Vocalelli, 2017).

Green marketing is attracting significant attention as companies increasingly develop strategies to ensure their survival by creating green products in response to a growing base of eco-conscious consumers, stricter government regulations, and the rising momentum of environmental campaigns advocating for a green economy (Alabdali, 2019; Grunert, 2013). Manufacturers and retailers communicate product sustainability through signals aimed at certifying specific sustainable characteristics, known as *eco-labels*. These labels are designed to identify and differentiate products with positive environmental and social impacts while reducing uncertainty about the validity of consumers' green purchases (Darnall et al., 2018).

As noted by Atkinson and Rosenthal (2014), signaling theory—focused on how market participants address or mitigate information imbalances concerning the inherent quality of a person, product, or entity (Connelly et al., 2011)—offers a framework for understanding how eco-labels can validate the authenticity of environmental claims made by advertisers. Previous studies (e.g., Caswell & Mojduszka, 1996; Karstens & Belz, 2006; Thøgersen, 2010) have shown that eco-labels help transform experience attributes (qualities that consumers can assess only after use) or credence attributes (traits consumers cannot independently verify) into search attributes (features easily observable by consumers). Thus, eco-labels function as convenient information shortcuts (or heuristics) in the consumer's evaluation process and are used to influence consumers' purchasing decisions by providing assurances about the sustainability and ecological performance of products (Donato &

D'Aniello, 2022). Below are some of the key roles of eco-labels in the context of green marketing:

- **Reducing Information Asymmetry**: Eco-labels help bridge the information gap between producers and consumers regarding the environmental attributes of products. They provide verifiable and easily understandable information that enables consumers to make informed and conscious choices, reducing uncertainty about the environmental performance of products (Delmas & Lessem, 2016).
- **Building Consumer Trust**: Eco-labels can increase consumer trust in environmental claims of products. When an eco-label is issued by an independent third-party organization, consumers are more likely to believe that the product actually meets the stated environmental standards, thereby mitigating fears of greenwashing (Nuttavuthisit & Thøgersen, 2017; Testa et al., 2015).
- **Product Differentiation:** Eco-labels allow companies to differentiate their products from competitors. In a market increasingly sensitive to environmental issues, eco-labels can be a key differentiating factor that attracts environmentally conscious consumers, helping to build a competitive advantage (Papadas et al., 2017).
- **Promoting Sustainability**: Eco-labels not only influence consumer choices, but also promote sustainable production practices. Companies that seek to obtain an eco-label often need to meet stringent environmental criteria, thus encouraging the adoption of more sustainable technologies and processes (Dangelico & Vocalelli, 2017).
- **Education and Awareness**: Eco-labels educate consumers about environmental issues and raise awareness of sustainable practices. Through the use of eco-labels, consumers become more aware of the environmental impact of their purchases and can be encouraged to make more sustainable choices (Parguel et al., 2015).
- **Supporting Government Policies:** Eco-labels support government policies that promote environmental sustainability. Many governments encourage the use of eco-labels as part of their strategies to reduce overall environmental impact and promote sustainability at national and international levels (Alabdali, 2019).
- **Corporate Social Responsibility (CSR):** Eco-labels are an important component of corporate social responsibility (CSR) strategies. They demonstrate a company's commitment to responsible environmental

practices and can enhance corporate reputation, increasing customer trust and loyalty (Pizzetti et al., 2021).

In summary, eco-labels play a pivotal role in bridging the gap between consumer knowledge and the environmental performance of products, offering a credible and easily interpretable tool that enhances trust, fosters product differentiation, and promotes sustainable practices across industries.

3   GREEN MARKETING SIGNALS: TYPES OF ECO-LABELS

Eco-labels do not function in isolation; they are often supported by broader environmental management frameworks that guide organizations in achieving and maintaining sustainable practices. These frameworks play a crucial role in ensuring that the environmental claims behind eco-labels are not only credible but also grounded in rigorous processes and established standards.

At the heart of these frameworks is the Environmental Management System (EMS),[1] which serves as a structured approach for organizations to manage their environmental responsibilities. EMS enables organizations to systematically identify, monitor, and mitigate their environmental impacts, thereby fostering a culture of continuous improvement.

The ISO 14000[2] family of standards provides a comprehensive framework for effective environmental management, with ISO 14001[3] specifically outlining the requirements for establishing and maintaining an EMS. This standard emphasizes key principles, such as continuous improvement, legal compliance, and stakeholder engagement. Organizations that adhere to ISO 14001 can develop a structured approach to managing their environmental impacts, setting measurable objectives, and implementing strategies to achieve these goals.

In addition to ISO 14001, the Eco-Management and Audit Scheme (EMAS)[4] builds upon this framework, offering a more stringent set of requirements for organizations seeking to enhance their environmental

---

[1] https://www.epa.gov/ems.

[2] https://www.iso.org/standards/popular/iso-14000-family.

[3] https://www.iso.org/standard/60857.html.

[4] https://green-business.ec.europa.eu/emas_en.

performance. EMAS incorporates the principles of ISO 14001 but goes further by mandating additional obligations, such as transparency in public reporting and increased oversight by regulatory authorities. This emphasis on public accountability ensures that organizations are not only compliant with environmental regulations but are also committed to openly communicating their environmental impacts and improvements to stakeholders and the public.

Both ISO 14001 and EMAS play an integral role in enhancing the credibility of eco-labels. Organizations that implement these systems can obtain certifications that validate their environmental claims, thereby reinforcing the integrity of the eco-labels they use. This connection ensures that eco-labels serve as reliable indicators of a company's genuine commitment to sustainable practices, rather than merely serving as marketing tools. When consumers see an eco-label, they can be assured that the product has undergone a rigorous evaluation process aligned with internationally recognized environmental management standards.

Eco-labels can be categorized into three main types, as defined within the ISO 14020 subset of the ISO 14000 series (Prieto-Sandoval et al., 2016): Type I, Type II, and Type III.

Each type serves a distinct purpose and provides different levels of assurance regarding environmental claims.

- *Type I*. This category includes voluntary environmental labels based on a pass-fail multicriteria system that analyzes the entire product life cycle, indicating overall environmental performance. If any of the criteria are not met, the product does not receive the label. These labels are also subject to external certification by an independent body according to the requirements of ISO 14024.[5] They provide straightforward documents with basic environmental information, often featuring simple, recognizable symbols like leaves, flowers, or animals to represent eco-friendliness. Common colors include green, blue, and earth tones to signify sustainability and nature. Text is minimal, focusing on the certification body and the eco-label's logo, without detailed product information. Examples of Type I labels include "Fairtrade" and "EU Ecolabel" certifications.

---

[5] https://www.iso.org/standard/72458.html.

- *Type II*. This category includes labels consisting of self-declarations made by manufacturers and businesses. According to ISO 14021,[6] the applicant can declare the environmental quality of their product without predefined criteria, reference marks, or quality controls. However, this declaration must always be verifiable and never misleading. Other restrictions include avoiding vague or ambiguous claims such as "environmentally friendly" or "more sustainable." Instead, verifiable terms like "made with x% recycled material" are permitted. Type II labels may include logos or symbols but are generally less formal than Type I, often using green or blue tones to evoke nature and eco-friendliness. These labels consist of self-declared claims by manufacturers, featuring specific statements like "recyclable," "biodegradable," or "carbon neutral," but without third-party verification. Examples of Type II labels include claims like "Recyclable" and "Compostable."

- *Type III*. This category is also known as Environmental Product Declarations (EPDs), it is defined by ISO 14025[7] and comprehends third-party verified within established programs. Prepared based on Life Cycle Assessment (LCA) using predefined criteria, EPDs are generally more complex, containing a range of information from various aspects of the product's supply chain. Type III labels are comparable to nutritional labels on food products and can be used to compare products based on strict guidelines set by relevant standards. Type III labels are the most suitable for communicating a product's environmental credentials to businesses, public entities, and informed consumers. They can be viewed as the product's ecological footprint, offering more comprehensive information than Type I and Type II labels. These labels are typically more technical and data-driven, often featuring tables, charts, or numerical data. The design is neutral and professional, focusing on presenting objective information rather than relying on symbolic visuals. Examples of Type III labels include EcoLeaf (Japan) and Product Environmental Footprint (PEF) (European Union).

---

[6] https://www.iso.org/standard/66652.html.

[7] https://www.iso.org/standard/38131.html.

Table 1 The three eco-label types

Criterion	Type I	Type II	Type III
Regulation	ISO 14024	ISO 14021	ISO 14025
Target Group	B2C	B2C and B2B	B2C and B2B
Third-party verification	Yes	No	Yes
Type	Voluntary	Voluntary	Voluntary
Design	Simple icons, green/ blue tones, minimal text	Simple icons, self-declared claims, green/blue tones	Ecological footprint, technical data, tables
Examples	"Fairtrade" "EU Ecolabel"	"Recyclable" "Compostable" claims	EcoLeaf (Japan), Product Environmental Footprint (PEF) (European Union)

Table 1 synthesizes the main distinctions between the three types of eco-labels

In addition to the ISO classification, eco-labels can be further distinguished into broader categories:

- *Environmental Eco-Labels* focus on the overall environmental impact of products, emphasizing sustainability and the reduction of negative environmental effects. These labels include Type I and Type III certifications, providing credible information to consumers about a product's sustainability performance.
- *Ecological Eco-Labels* highlight products produced using environmentally friendly methods or materials, often emphasizing organic or natural production practices. This category can be seen as a subset of environmental eco-labels, concentrating specifically on ecological integrity.
- *Fair Trade Labels* prioritize social and economic criteria, ensuring that products are made under fair labor conditions and that producers receive equitable compensation. While they may also consider environmental aspects, their primary focus is on social justice and promoting sustainable livelihoods.

Each of these categories plays a vital role in guiding consumer choices toward more sustainable options. The following sections will analyze each category in detail, exploring their characteristics and contributions to the broader goal of sustainability.

3.1   Environmental Eco-Labels

Environmental product labels aim to inform consumers about the environmental performance of a product or service as transparently as possible. These labels promote the dissemination of "green" and sustainable products by involving consumers, administrations, and businesses. Positioned on product packaging, they provide environmental information to consumers in a visible manner. Prominent examples include:

- *The European Ecolabel*: This label is valid in all European Union countries and Switzerland. It is awarded to packaging and products that do not harm the environment but do not apply to agri-food products, pharmaceuticals, or automotive sector products.
- *The Forest Stewardship Council (FSC)*: This label ensures that the wood used in the production of products comes from sustainably managed forests.
- *The Nordic Swan*: This label uses the same criteria as the European ecological quality mark, although it is stricter on organic matters.
- *Process Chlorine Free (PCF)*: This label ensures that the chemical bleaching of paper is done without the use of chlorine-based chemicals.
- *BPA Free*: This label identifies products that do not contain bisphenol A (BPA), a toxic organic compound released by many plastics, especially polycarbonate containers commonly used for food contact.
- *The Möbius Strip*: This symbol indicates whether a product is recyclable. In some cases, a percentage may appear in the center of the logo, indicating the proportion of recycled materials used to make the product. It is a universal logo found in many countries, though some countries use variations.
- *The Marine Stewardship Council (MSC)*: This label confirms that the fish comes from sustainable and environmentally respectful fishing practices.

- *Paper by Nature*: This label promotes certain eco-friendly practices in the stationery industry (for visual stimuli, see ecolabelindex.com).

Despite being used in different contexts and on various products, these labels often share common features. For instance, the color green is frequently used to convey the idea of an environmentally friendly product. Additionally, natural symbols such as stylized leaves and trees are common. Through the use of the color green and nature-related symbols, consumers are almost subconsciously informed about the environmental characteristics of these products.

In summary, environmental product labels are vital for promoting sustainable consumption by clearly communicating key environmental information to consumers and fostering collective commitment to sustainability.

3.2   Ecological Eco-Labels

Ecological labels play a crucial role in the global production and commercial landscape. They not only signify adherence to environmental and animal welfare standards but also assure consumers of the healthiness of the products. These labels indicate that the production process avoids pesticides and includes natural animal rearing practices, explicitly rejecting intensive farming methods (Annunziata & Vecchio, 2016). Notable examples of ecological eco-labels are:

- *Euroleaf Ecolabel (EU)*: This is a European label that certifies a product comes from organic farming. When this certification is on a product's packaging, the buyer can be assured that it contains no synthetic chemicals and has been produced naturally. Its use is mandatory for organic products sold within the European Union.
- *Ecocert*: This label is most commonly found on beauty creams, but its scope is expanding to include organic cosmetics, as well as textiles and fair trade products.
- *COSMEBIO*: This label guarantees that the cosmetics purchased are produced using processes that respect both people and the environment and do not contain GMOs, colorants, petroleum derivatives, or synthetic fragrances.

- *Nature&Progres*: This label is one of the most stringent eco-quality labels in terms of compliance with the specifications and standards established by the association.
- *AB Certification*: This French organic label indicates that a product meets strict organic farming standards. It ensures that agricultural practices are environmentally friendly and that the product contains no synthetic additives or chemicals. The AB logo is recognized across Europe and is essential for organic products sold in France.

These labels indicate that products adhere to defined environmental standards, supporting sustainable practices and minimizing environmental impact. To qualify as ecological, a product must meet rigorous criteria, such as the exclusion of chemical substances and a completely segregated supply chain from conventional products. Europe, particularly countries like Italy, Germany, and France, is a leading producer of organic raw materials, which are exported throughout the continent. The production, labeling, and control of organic products are regulated by standardized EU regulations. Similar to environmental labels, ecological or organic labels often feature common design elements, such as the color green to symbolize eco-friendliness and natural symbols like leaves and trees.

In summary, ecological labels not only promote sustainable agricultural practices but also provide consumers with assurance regarding the ecological integrity and health benefits of the products they purchase.

3.3   Fair Trade Eco-Labels

Fair Trade is a well-established system designed to ensure fair prices for producers. This concept has gained prominence with globalization and is now embedded in numerous commercial agreements where businesses in developed countries purchase from and guarantee prices for producers in developing nations. The Fair Trade (FT) eco-label aims to help producers in these countries secure better trading conditions (Ruggeri et al., 2021).

The International Fair Trade Association (IFAT) defines Fair Trade as *"a trading partnership, based on dialogue, transparency, and respect, that seeks greater equity in international trade"* and *"contributes to sustainable development by offering better trading conditions and securing the rights of marginalized producers and workers."* Fair Trade organizations support producers by keeping them informed about changes in international trade regulations and are bolstered by consumer backing (Grankvist et al., 2007).

They ensure socially responsible production and worker protection and can be displayed either prominently or discreetly on product packaging. Various labeling initiatives operate under different names, such as the World Fair Trade Organization, Max Havelaar, and Fair Ecocert (Mondoffice® Informa, 2020[8]).

According to the European Fair Trade Association (ETFA),[9] Fair Trade labeling organizations are present in 14 European countries, as well as in Canada, the United States, and Japan. In Europe, one of the most recognized examples is the Max Havelaar label (Loureiro & Lotade, 2005). These labels often feature similar design elements, such as the use of green and blue colors and stylized images of people, and are applied in various contexts. Noteworthy examples of Fair Trade eco-labels include:

- *Fair Trade International (FLO)* Certification: This certification ensures that producers meet rigorous Fair Trade standards, which include fair wages, safe working conditions, and environmentally sustainable practices. FLO coordinates and promotes Fair Trade standards internationally and works to strengthen Fair Trade producer organizations worldwide.
- *Fair Ecocert*: This certification guarantees that at least 5% of the ingredients in the product composition come from Fair Trade. This can apply to food products, textiles, as well as the cosmetics industry.
- *World Fair Organization* Label: Its purpose is to enable producers to improve their livelihoods and communities through ethical trade.

Ultimately, Fair Trade eco-labels not only promote ethical consumption but also empower producers in developing countries by ensuring equitable trading conditions and fostering sustainable development practices.

---

[8] https://www.mondoffice.com/mondoffice-informa/consigli-pratici/guida-pratica-alle-certificazioni-e-alle-etichette-di-qualita-ecologica.html.

[9] http://www.european-fair-trade-association.org/efta/index.php.

4   ECO-LABEL STAKEHOLDERS: CONSUMERS, PRODUCERS, AND THIRD-PARTY ACTORS

The key stakeholders involved throughout the eco-label creation process, from the motivations behind a company seeking eco-friendly certification to the moment of purchasing sustainable products, include consumers, producers, and third-party entities responsible for certification approval (Horne, 2009).

4.1   Consumers

The first group of stakeholders refers to consumers who are pivotal in engaging with eco-labels to guide their purchase decisions toward environmentally aligned products rather than those from traditional or competing categories (Donato & Adıgüzel, 2022). A highly debated and analyzed topic is the willingness to pay (WTP) among consumers for such products. To justify paying a premium price for eco-labeled items, consumers need to be aware of the quality associated with these eco-friendly products. Research has shown that younger consumers and those more concerned about worker safety are more inclined to pay a premium, for instance, for apples labeled as being produced under fair and safe labor conditions (McCluskey & Loureiro, 2003). Once consumers are aware of the benefits, they tend to be willing to pay a premium for socially responsible goods (Donato & Adıgüzel, 2022). In particular, green consumers prioritize environmental factors, such as resource efficiency and product recyclability, when making purchasing decisions (Testa et al., 2015). However, negative consumer perceptions of green-labeled products can arise due to factors such as ineffective marketing strategies, higher prices, inconsistent product performance, and, most notably, mistrust (Hameed & Waris, 2018). Addressing consumer perceptions is essential, as environmental knowledge and awareness play a critical role in green market segmentation (Peattie, 2001; Straughan & Roberts, 1999).

Peattie (2001) developed a segmentation model that categorizes the market into three key groups based on the degree of conscious environmental concern among consumers (see Fig. 1).

The first group, "*Consistent Ecologists,*" involves well-informed consumers who are consistently committed to environmental sustainability in their purchasing decisions. The second group, "*Grey Consumers,*" is indifferent to environmental concerns, more skeptical

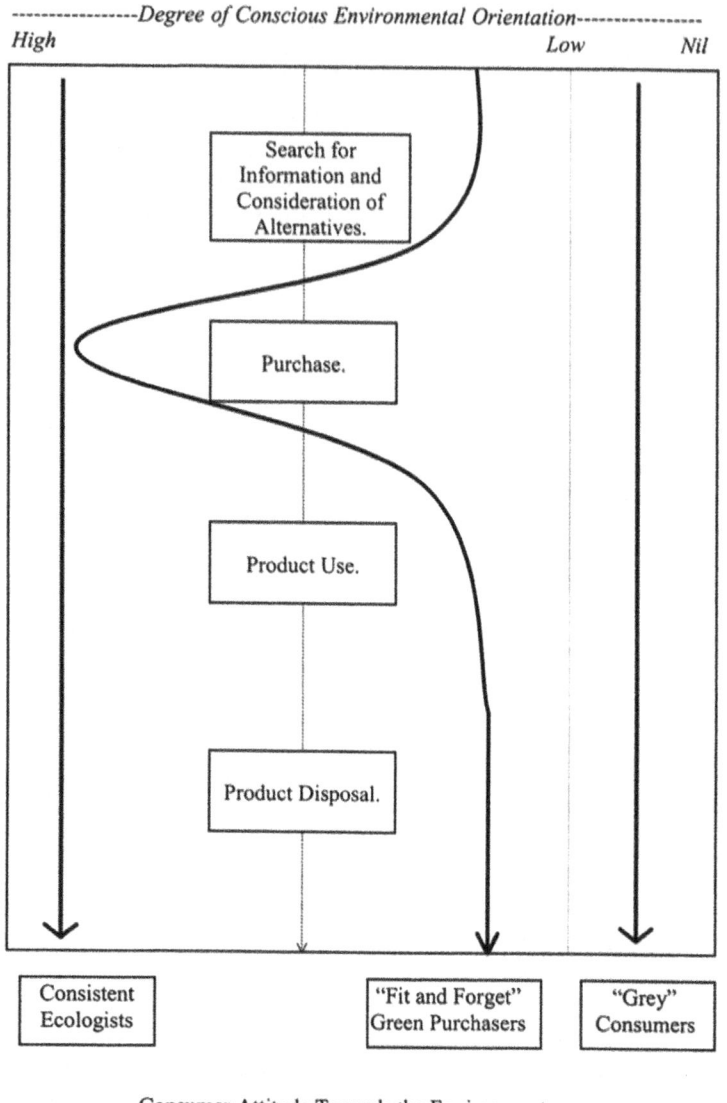

-----------------Degree of Conscious Environmental Orientation-----------------

High   Low   Nil

Search for
Information and
Consideration of
Alternatives.

Purchase.

Product Use.

Product Disposal.

Consistent
Ecologists

"Fit and Forget"
Green Purchasers

"Grey"
Consumers

----------------Consumer Attitude Towards the Environment--------------------

Fig. 1 A simplified model of environmental orientation during the consumption process (*Source* Peattie K., 2001)

about environmental issues, and shows little interest in eco-labeled products. Lastly, *"Fit and Forget Purchasers"* engage with eco-friendly products but require further education, making them an ideal target for raising environmental awareness. While they do buy ecological products, they need more information both before and after making a purchase.

As further analyzed by Peattie (2001) and earlier by Ottman and Books (1998), the needs of green consumers can be categorized into four main areas: the need for information, the need for control, the need to make a difference, and the need to maintain their current lifestyles. Green consumers are often driven by a desire for detailed and transparent information about the product's environmental impact. They seek control over their choices, preferring products that allow them to contribute meaningfully to environmental sustainability. Additionally, they have a strong desire to make a difference by supporting environmentally responsible practices, as they believe their purchasing decisions can lead to positive change. At the same time, they aim to maintain their current lifestyles, looking for products that integrate seamlessly into their daily routines without requiring significant sacrifices.

In this context, Peattie (2001) developed an approach to understanding green consumer behavior during the purchasing phase, focusing on two key variables: the degree of compromise required and the confidence in the product's environmental benefits (see Fig. 2). The matrix comprises four quadrants that reflect distinct consumer purchasing behaviors. In the *Feelgood Purchases* quadrant (high confidence, high compromise), consumers believe strongly in the environmental benefits of products and are willing to make trade-offs, often choosing brands or products clearly involved in sustainability, like The Body Shop, or organic cotton clothing. Conversely, *Win–win Purchases* (low compromise, high confidence) consist of consumers who feel assured about the environmental impact of their choices but seek products that do not compromise on quality or cost, such as Café Direct coffee and recycled paper products. The *Why Bother? Purchases* quadrant (high compromise, low confidence) includes consumers who are skeptical about the effectiveness of their purchases yet are willing to compromise, opting for products like green cars. Lastly, *Why Not? Purchases* (low compromise, low confidence) reflect consumers who lack confidence in the environmental benefits and are unwilling to make trade-offs, often choosing items like unleaded petrol or detergent refills.

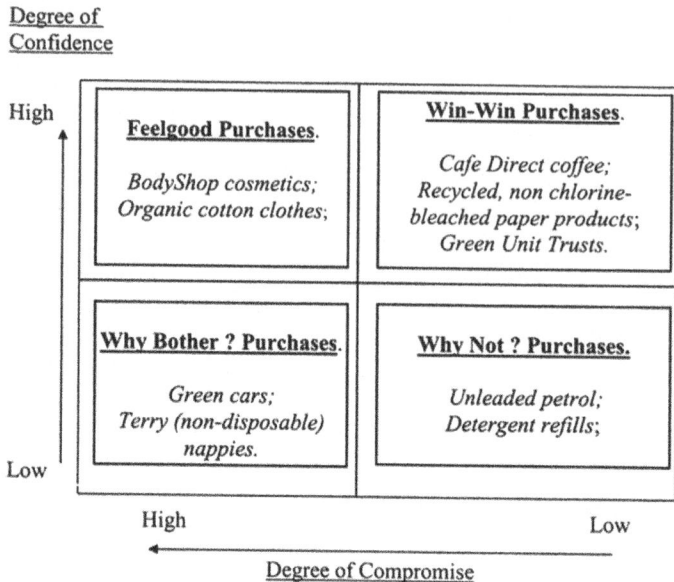

Fig. 2   The green purchase perception matrix (*Source* Peattie K., 2001)

This matrix provides valuable insights into consumer behavior, enabling businesses to tailor their marketing strategies to address diverse motivations and attitudes toward sustainable consumption. Initially, green marketing promoted "win–win" products that combined premium pricing with environmental benefits. However, recent strategies emphasize creating affordable, environmentally superior products without sacrificing technical quality. It is crucial for consumers to find these compromises acceptable. Research indicates that even the most eco-conscious consumers are increasingly unwilling to pay more for greener goods but are open to altering their buying patterns. Buyers require assurance that environmental issues are genuine, that the product outperforms competitors in eco-friendliness, and that their purchase will make a tangible difference. However, skepticism remains high, with consumers expressing greater trust in environmental groups than in manufacturers regarding product claims. The success of green products often hinges on their positioning within the win–win quadrant, offering clear environmental benefits with minimal compromises. Products achieving this balance, such as detergent refills, tend to perform well in the market. Conversely, items requiring greater sacrifices, like non-disposable nappies, must instill higher confidence in their environmental benefits. For example, Body Shop products, despite their higher prices, maintain credibility due to a strong environmental reputation, while non-disposable nappies have seen consumer confidence erode due to conflicting research on their environmental advantages.

D'Souza (2004) presents another type of segmentation (see Fig. 3) which is a two-dimensional model describing the cognitive perspective of environmental products. This refers to the information conveyed through eco-labels, which may include symbols, codes, signs, or informative texts that consumers use to identify eco-friendly products. The vertical axis represents perceived product benefits and risks, while the horizontal axis differentiates between cognitive and non-cognitive perspectives, capturing two key dimensions of consumer sentiment.

On the right side of the model are emerging green consumers and conventional consumers, who tend to be less concerned with environmental issues and typically prefer other mainstream brands. On the opposite side are environmentally conscious consumers, who consider the broader environmental impact of products and move beyond merely assessing the risks associated with purchasing them. This two-dimensional

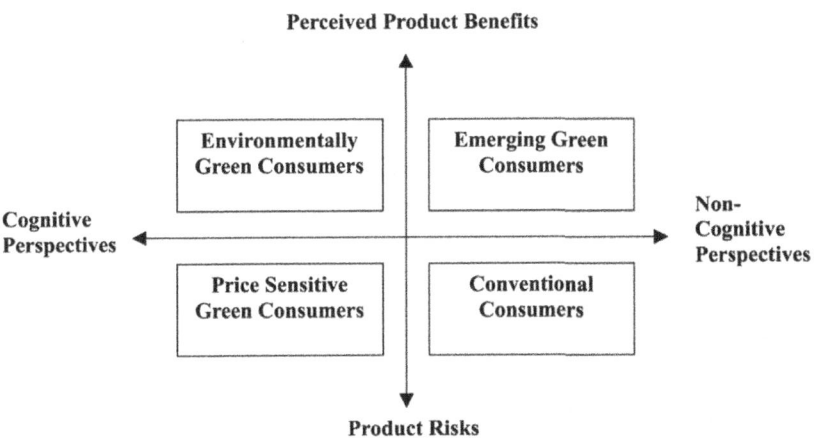

Fig. 3 A two-dimensional model of the cognitive perspective on environmental products (*Source* D'Souza C., 2004)

approach aims to capture the complexity of consumer behavior when choosing environmentally friendly products. On the basis of these two dimensions, the model identifies four consumer segments:

- *Green Consumers*: These consumers are highly environmentally conscious and consistently choose green products. They carefully review label information for environmental attributes, representing a group of proactive buyers seeking products with strong environmental credentials.
- *Emerging Green Consumers*: While they recognize the benefits of green products, these consumers are not always motivated to purchase them consistently. Their brand choices are often driven by other factors, and they show limited interest in environmental information, making eco-labels less impactful on their decisions.
- *Price-Sensitive Green Consumers*: These individuals are aware of and scrutinize eco-labels, understanding the associated product risks. However, they are highly price-conscious and may hesitate to pay a premium for eco-friendly products.
- *Conventional Consumers*: This segment does not prioritize environmental considerations and may view the risks of green products as comparable to those of non-green products. They generally disregard the potential benefits of eco-friendly products.

4.2   Producers

The second group of stakeholders is the producers, who have increasingly recognized the importance of targeting environmentally conscious consumers (e.g., Asche et al., 2015). Marketers are now working diligently to promote green products to boost sales while aligning with the company's broader sustainability goals. However, not all companies have been successful in translating consumer environmental concerns into tangible sales growth. This challenge underscores the importance of understanding market demands and adopting long-term focused strategies to effectively reach eco-conscious consumers (e.g., Annunziata et al., 2019; Eldesouky et al., 2020). Such strategies span multiple dimensions of marketing, from generating demand for sustainable products to understanding the psychological factors that influence consumer acceptance of green products. These factors include consumer attitudes toward eco-labels, the perceived value of environmentally friendly products, and demographic variables such as age, income, and education level, which play a role in shaping consumer decision-making and product preferences (Hameed & Waris, 2018).

Due to the unpredictable and often limited demand for green products, many organizations have adopted a cautious "wait-and-see" approach, hesitating to invest fully in environmental product lines. Some companies, particularly smaller and medium-sized enterprises (SMEs), simply extend their traditional product offerings with environmentally friendly options rather than fully integrating sustainability into their business models. For these SMEs, the complexity and resource demands of implementing and maintaining environmentally sustainable standards— such as establishing reverse logistics systems for waste management—can seem overwhelming and exceed their financial and operational capacities (Bhaskaran et al., 2006). To overcome these challenges and gain a competitive advantage, manufacturers can leverage large distribution networks, enabling them to reach a broader consumer base. In addition to widening their reach, these companies can enhance the perceived quality and credibility of their green products by running informational campaigns, offering special promotions, and collaborating with other brands in co-marketing initiatives. Synergies across different product categories, such as food, detergents, tissue paper, fabrics, and paints, can also strengthen their ecological brand presence and increase consumer trust in their sustainability efforts (Testa et al., 2015).

4.3 Third-Party Entities

Lastly, third-party certification entities play a crucial role by validating a product's environmental claims, especially when consumers are concerned about environmental impact but lack the information or means to assess it independently. The image and credibility of these third-party entities are essential in fostering consumer trust in such cases. However, the presence of multiple accreditation sources can sometimes confuse consumers and even undermine the credibility of the information provided (Bhaskaran et al., 2006). In contrast, in markets where consumers are well-informed about environmental issues, third-party certification becomes a highly effective tool for enhancing competitiveness. By providing greater environmental assurances and clear market information, these certifications boost consumer confidence, which, in turn, positively impacts competitiveness and revenue. Marketing campaigns that effectively leverage eco-labels can significantly influence consumer responsibility and improve attitudes toward purchasing environmentally friendly products (Testa et al., 2015).

There is a clear distinction between brands certified by independent third parties and other forms of self-regulation. As thoroughly analyzed by Van Amstel et al. (2008), many self-regulatory mechanisms fail to separate legislative functions (standard setting) from execution (certification) by independent third-party bodies. To break the information monopoly held by producers, ecological quality brands often involve two independent third parties: a standardization body (SB) that sets the environmentally friendly production standards and a certification body (CB) that ensures compliance with these standards. An Accreditation Body (AB) oversees the certification body, ensuring its independence, impartiality, confidentiality, and integrity. This structure guarantees consumer trust by assuring them that producers are adhering to the necessary environmental standards (Van Amstel et al., 2008).

Figure 4 illustrates this "certification triangle," which highlights how these entities—SB, CB, and AB—work together to ensure independent and credible oversight of producers' adherence to environmental standards (see also De Graaff, 1996). The continuous arrows in the figure represent a regulatory relationship: a contract where the seller/producer (S—Seller) agrees to comply with the standards of the eco-quality brand, established by the SB, or contracts involving the CB's control over the seller and the AB's control over the CB. Meanwhile, the dashed arrows illustrate various forms of communication, such as written exchanges, meetings, or participation in the certification process. For instance, the seller (S) informs the buyer (B) about the product carrying the eco-label or certificate. Occasionally, a seller may participate in advising or being part of the SB itself. Coordination between the SB and CB is essential for setting the standards and defining the inspection processes needed to verify compliance with these standards. Additionally, the SB and CB collaborate to ensure that these standards are clearly defined and effectively enforced. This certification structure helps ensure that products meet environmental criteria, enhancing transparency and consumer trust.

The separation of powers is fundamental to providing assurances throughout the planning and implementation phases of ecological brands.

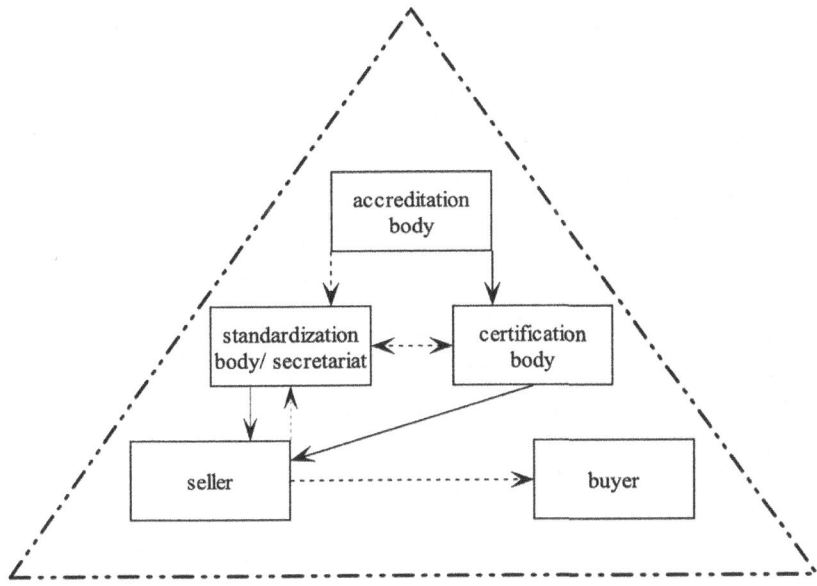

Fig. 4 Certification Triangle (*Source* Van Amstel et al., 2008)

During the planning phase, an independent third party oversees standard-ization, while another independent third party verifies whether producers have adhered to these standards during the implementation phase. Once successful verification occurs, the certification body issues a conformity statement, certifying that the producer has complied with the standards. However, it is important to note that there is no independent third party monitoring the actual outcomes during the production phase of an ecological quality brand. Ecological brands do not guarantee that a product itself meets certain environmental standards; rather, they certify that the production process complies with them (Van Amstel et al., 2008). This certification structure ensures transparency and consumer trust by clearly separating the stages of standard setting, compliance veri-fication, and certification, thus enhancing the credibility of ecological quality brands.

5   Eco-Labels in Action: Business Cases Driving Consumer Preference and Market Success

Eco-labels have emerged as a critical tool for companies across various sectors, particularly in the food industry, where consumer demand for sustainable and ethically sourced products has significantly increased (e.g., Donato & Adıgüzel, 2022; Grunert et al., 2014). These certifications not only assure consumers of the environmental and social responsibility of the products they purchase, but also play a crucial role in shaping brand perception, driving sales, and fostering customer loyalty. The present section explores how leading companies such as Nestlé, Unilever, Findus, and IKEA have effectively implemented eco-labels within their product lines and the substantial impact these initiatives have had on their market performance.

5.1   Nestlé

Nestlé, one of the largest food and beverage companies globally,[10] recognized early on the importance of sustainability in consumer decision-making. The company's KitKat brand, a staple in its confectionery portfolio, became one of the first to adopt the Rainforest Alliance Certified seal (i.e., Type I environmental sustainability eco-label promotes also social and economic sustainability in agriculture and forestry. It ensures that products are produced using methods that protect ecosystems, wildlife, and communities. Certified farms adhere to rigorous standards, including responsible land use, conservation practices, and fair labor conditions). This certification guarantees that the cocoa used in KitKat is sourced from farms that adhere to stringent environmental, social, and economic standards. The decision to feature the Rainforest Alliance certification was not merely a marketing strategy, but a reflection of Nestlé's broader commitment to sustainable sourcing and corporate responsibility.[11] Launched in 2022, this program incentivizes farmers to engage in activities such as enrolling children in school and diversifying incomes.

---

[10] https://vinut.com.vn/2023/blogs/top-10-largest-food-and-beverage-companies/#:~:text=Nestl%C3%A9%20is%20the%20largest%20food,operates%20in%20191%20countries%20worldwide.

[11] https://www.nestle.co.uk/en-gb/ask-nestle/products-brands/answers/kitkat-moves-rainforest-alliance.

Currently, the program has reached over 10,000 families in Côte d'Ivoire and aims to impact 160,000 families globally by 2030. Nestlé's efforts include achieving full traceability and physical segregation of the cocoa used, ensuring high traceability standards. The "Breaks for Good" KitKat, featuring cocoa from this program, will be available across Europe in 2024.[12] The impact of Nestlé using Rainforest Alliance certification for its chocolate was profound. According to Rousseau (2015), chocolate using this type of label is more likely to influence consumer choice than pure organic labels. For most consumers, the organic label seems to become superfluous when selecting a self-indulgent treat such as chocolate. Therefore, the Rainforest Alliance certification has the potential to significantly boost KitKat's sales. The eco-label can serve as a powerful differentiator in the crowded chocolate market, where consumers are increasingly looking for products that align with their values. This strategic move by Nestlé underscores the effectiveness of eco-labels in enhancing product appeal and driving consumer preference, particularly among ethically minded consumers who are willing to pay a premium for sustainable products.

5.2 Unilever

Unilever, another global leader in the food and beverage industry, has similarly harnessed the power of eco-labels to drive growth and strengthen its brand. For many of Unilever's brands, third-party certification labels on product packaging play a role in storytelling about the source of ingredients and have done for many years. For example, the Ben & Jerries brand prominently displays the international Fairtrade Mark (Type I Fair Trade label that guarantees fair trading practices for farmers and workers in developing countries). It ensures they receive fair prices, decent working conditions, and a premium for community development projects on its ice cream products and uses the label to help it tell the consumer the story of where its cocoa comes from. On the Ben & Jerry's website, there are numerous stories highlighting the experiences of farmers and the benefits of Fair Trade to them and their communities. Unilever sees certifications that support its sustainable sourcing story as complementary to providing carbon footprint information and will continue to use both going forward, in addition to broader sustainability communications.

---

[12] https://www.confectioneryproduction.com/news/41178/nestle-extends-sustainable-paper-based-packaging-for-key-quality-street-kitkat-series/.

In particular, the company introduced carbon footprint labels (Type II environmental label indicating that the total amount of greenhouse gases emitted directly or indirectly by a product or service throughout its life cycle) on its products for the first time in 2021, marking a key moment in the shift to label products with their environmental impact. In particular, Unilever, which has 75,000 products, including Magnum ice cream, Pot Noodle, Marmite, and Hellmann's mayonnaise, applied the carbon footprint label to 30,000 of these products in a select range.

Previously, carbon footprint labels had been used only by plant-based companies, such as Quorn Foods and Oatly. Marc Engel, Unilever's global head of supply chain, said: "*Our market research shows that younger consumers, especially, are very impacted by climate change and are keen to use their buying behavior to send a message. We intend to roll out carbon labels on our entire product range over the next two to five years and believe it will transform not only the actions of consumers but also those of the thousands of businesses in our supply chain as well.*"[13]

Today, with climate change rising sharply up the public's agenda, consumers appear particularly sensitive to these information (Bayes et al., 2023). A 2020 survey by the Carbon Trust, which launched one of the world's first carbon footprint certification schemes, showed that almost two-thirds of adults in the UK support carbon labels, with around 80 percent backing them in France, Italy, and Spain. A recent EU study reported that 57 percent of consumers in the bloc were receptive to environmental claims when making purchase decisions.[14] Unilever's move was welcomed by the government as well as early adopters.

5.3   Findus

Findus, a leading European brand in the frozen food sector, has successfully leveraged eco-labels to strengthen its market position. The Marine Stewardship Council (MSC) certification (Type I environmental label certifying sustainable fishing practices, ensuring seafood is sourced from healthy fish populations and eco-friendly methods), which Findus has adopted for its seafood products, guarantees that the fish is sourced from

---

[13] https://packaging360.in/news/unilever-breakthrough-as-food-industry-giant-introduces-carbon-footprint-labels-on-food/.

[14] https://www.carbontrust.com/en-eu/our-work-and-impact/guides-reports-and-tools/product-carbon-footprint-labelling-consumer-research-2020.

sustainable fisheries that are managed to maintain healthy fish populations and minimize environmental impact. The MSC label, recognized globally as the gold standard for sustainable fishing (Bronnmann et al., 2023), has been instrumental in driving consumer preference and boosting sales of Findus products. From April 2022, the value of MSC-labeled sales has increased by up to 9%.[15]

Furthermore, at the retail level, studies in Germany and the UK have reported price premiums for MSC-certified seafood of up to 30% (Asche & Bronnmann, 2017; Asche et al., 2015; Sogn-Grundvåg et al., 2013, 2014), as well as for other certifications like the Aquaculture Stewardship Council (Asche et al., 2021). The MSC certification not only has the potential to boost sales but also reinforces Findus' reputation as a brand committed to sustainability, further distinguishing it from competitors in the frozen food market.

5.4   IKEA

IKEA, known globally for its affordable and stylish furniture, has also made significant strides in integrating sustainability into its food offerings. The company's decision to adopt the Aquaculture Stewardship Council (ASC) certification (Type I environmental label certifying responsible aquaculture practices, promoting sustainable seafood production while minimizing environmental impact and supporting local communities) for the salmon served in its in-store restaurants is a prime example of this commitment.[16] The ASC certification ensures that the seafood is farmed in a way that minimizes environmental and social impacts, aligning with IKEA's broader sustainability goals. The decision to offer ASC-certified salmon was part of IKEA's strategy to make sustainable food choices accessible to its millions of customers. Also in this case, the ASC label not only has the potentiality to enhance IKEA's reputation as a leader in sustainability but also to lead to an increase in sales of its salmon dishes, particularly among customers who are increasingly aware of the environmental impact of their food choices. By offering ASC-certified seafood, IKEA can strengthen its brand image as a company that cares about

---

[15] https://www.msc.org/media-centre/press-releases/press-release/msc-sets-out-strategy-for-expansion-of-sustainable-seafood.

[16] https://asc-aqua.org/farmers-stories/ikea-sustainable-seafood/.

the environment and offers sustainable choices across its product range, including in its food offerings.

These cases collectively demonstrate the powerful role that eco-labels can play in driving sales, enhancing brand reputation, and fostering customer loyalty across various sectors within the food industry. As consumer awareness of environmental and social issues continues to grow, the adoption of eco-labels will likely become increasingly important for companies looking to differentiate themselves in the marketplace and build long-term customer relationships. The success of these initiatives by Nestlé, Unilever, Findus, and IKEA underscores the strategic value of eco-labels in today's competitive market environment, where sustainability is no longer just a trend but a key factor in consumer decision-making.

6   Eco-Labels in Green Consumerism

The business cases previously discussed highlight the practical application and success of eco-labels in driving sustainability and brand sales across various sectors. However, the effectiveness of eco-labels goes beyond individual cases, shaping broader consumer behavior and market trends. Understanding the factors that influence the perception and credibility of eco-labels is crucial for their continued success in promoting environmental sustainable products. This section analyzes the challenges, benefits, and socio-demographic factors associated with eco-labels, along with the rising concerns of greenwashing, which threaten to undermine their impact.

Eco-labels play a crucial role in influencing consumer behavior, making them highly relevant to all stakeholders, including consumers, businesses, governments, and environmental groups (Dekhili & Akli Achabou, 2014; Sigurdsson et al., 2022; Sirieix et al., 2013). Despite their potential, understanding how eco-labels influence consumer decision-making remains a challenge due to the complexity of green demand. Green consumerism, defined as making purchasing decisions based on environmental or social criteria (Peattie, 1995), is shaped by various factors, but the exact determinants are still unclear. Economic theory suggests that consumer tastes and preferences, traditionally hard to model, play a role in green product demand (Celsi & Olson, 1988; Park & Young, 1986). Social psychologists further show that a person's eco-behavior is positively influenced by their level of environmental involvement and its specificity (Grankvist & Biel, 2001; Kokkinaki, 1997; Thøgersen,

2002). Involvement, interpreted as personal relevance, affects attention and comprehension, while environmental concern and perceived consumer effectiveness also significantly impact eco-behavior (Bamberg, 2003; Lee & Holden, 1999; Thøgersen, 1999, 2000, 2002). Norms and beliefs about social behaviors influence these eco-related actions as well (Ajzen et al., 2004; Hopper & Nielsen, 1991; Pretty & Ward, 2001; Stern, 2005). Socio-demographic characteristics have also been shown to play an important role in shaping eco-attitudes and behaviors, although the results have been mixed. Studies suggest that women tend to be more eco-conscious than men, possibly due to socialization patterns (Johnston et al., 2001; Loureiro et al., 2001; Zelezny et al., 2000). The effect of education varies, with some studies indicating a positive influence (Blend & van Ravenswaay, 1999) while others report negligible or negative impacts (Johnston et al., 2001; Moon et al., 2002). Age also presents mixed results, reflecting differences in information processing and time valuation (Clark et al., 2003; Moon et al., 2002; Rice, 2006; Roberts, 1996). Income, however, seems to have little effect on eco-behavior (Blend & van Ravenswaay, 1999; Loureiro et al., 2001; Moon et al., 2002).

Focusing on eco-label research, existing studies demonstrate that eco-labels engage stakeholders like governments, retailers, and environmental groups, helping signal a product's environmental attributes and reduce consumer uncertainty (Gulbrandsen, 2006; Rao et al., 1999; Thøgersen et al., 2010), and that can significantly influence purchasing decisions (Donato & Adıgüzel, 2022).

In particular, these labels serve as powerful tools for environmentally conscious consumers, especially in fast-moving consumer goods (FMCG) sectors such as coffee, wine, yogurt, and potato chips. These green tools have been found to enhance perceived product quality and justify the payment of premium prices (Lotz et al., 2013; Sörqvist et al., 2013, 2015; Wiedmann et al., 2014). However, these positive outcomes are contingent on the proper visibility of eco-labels (Markandya, 1997; Zarrilli et al., 1997). Moreover, the credibility and effectiveness of eco-labels are critical for fostering genuine green consumerism and addressing barriers such as misinterpretation and skepticism (Hemmelskamp & Brockmann, 1997; Morris, 1997).

Nonetheless, the adoption of eco-labels remains limited due to a lack of consumer awareness and understanding (Annunziata et al., 2019;

Eldesouky et al., 2020). A prominent challenge is the so-called "eco-penalty," where eco-labeled products are sometimes perceived as lower in quality compared to non-eco-labeled alternatives, especially in sectors like wine (Delmas & Lessem, 2017). This suggests that despite the environmental benefits, consumers might associate eco-labels with inferior quality, particularly when these products are priced higher or originate from regions perceived as lower in quality (Delmas & Lessem, 2017). Furthermore, eco-products are often viewed as inconvenient, costly, or of lesser quality (Grankvist & Biel, 2001; Stern, 1999). Negative pre-existing attitudes toward eco-products can also affect how consumers process new information (Fazio, 1986; Thøgersen, 1999, 2002; Thorson et al., 1995).

A significant obstacle to green consumerism is greenwashing, where companies make misleading or exaggerated environmental claims, undermining consumer trust in green products and eco-labels (Du, 2015) and making consumers wary of paying a premium for products marketed as environmentally friendly. Despite increased government penalties, the prevalence of misleading environmental claims persists, with companies often using vague language that obscures poor environmental performance (Parguel et al., 2015; Pizzetti et al., 2021). Such practices typically manifest in three forms: false claims, omission of important information, or ambiguous language, all of which erode confidence in green advertising (Parguel et al., 2015). As a result, consumer trust in eco-labels is at risk of being undermined. A 2020 European Commission study found that 53.3% of environmental claims were vague, misleading, or unfounded, and 40% lacked any substantiation,[17] which contributes to consumers perceiving these claims as unreliable and hesitating to make more sustainable purchasing decisions (Testa et al., 2015).

To counteract this, producers must offer clear, comprehensive, and easily understood information on their products' environmental attributes, as credible eco-labels enhance perceived credibility and help consumers identify eco-friendly options (Donato & D'Aniello, 2022; Teisl & Roe, 2005; Teisl, 2003).

In conclusion, while eco-labels are powerful tools for promoting sustainability and influencing consumer behavior, their effectiveness is constrained by issues like consumer awareness, perceptions of product

---

[17] https://ec.europa.eu/commission/presscorner/detail/en/ip_23_1692.

quality, and skepticism toward green claims. Given the obstacles to eco-label perceptions and understanding, it is crucial for these sustainable marketing tools to be effectively communicated through proper visual design. The next chapter will delve into the aesthetic dimensions and their effects on consumer perceptions.

References

Alabdali, N. H. (2019). Factors affecting the application of the concept of green marketing: An empirical study in Saudi Food Industry Companies. *International Journal of Business and Social Science, 10*(6), 43–53.

Ajzen, I., Brown, T. C., & Carvajal, F. (2004). Explaining the discrepancy between intentions and actions: The case of hypothetical bias in contingent valuation. *Personality and Social Psychology Bulletin, 30*(9), 1108–1121.

Annunziata, A., & Vecchio, R. (2016). Organic farming and sustainability in food choices: An analysis of consumer preference in Southern Italy. *Agriculture and Agricultural Science Procedia, 8*, 193–200.

Annunziata, A., Mariani, A., & Vecchio, R. (2019). Effectiveness of sustainability labels in guiding food choices: Analysis of visibility and understanding among young adults. *Sustainable Production and Consumption, 17*, 108–115.

Asche, F., & Bronnmann, J. (2017). Price premiums for ecolabelled seafood: MSC certification in Germany. *Australian Journal of Agricultural and Resource Economics, 61*(4), 576–589.

Asche, F., Bronnmann, J., & Cojocaru, A. L. (2021). The value of responsibly farmed fish: A hedonic price study of ASC-certified whitefish. *Ecological Economics, 188*, 107135.

Asche, F., Larsen, T.A., Smith, M.D., Sogn-Grundvåg, G., & Young, J.A. (2015). Pricing of eco-labels with retailer heterogeneity. *Food Policy, 53*, 82–93.

Atkinson, L., & Rosenthal, S. (2014). Signaling the green sell: The influence of eco-label source, argument specificity, and product involvement on consumer trust. *Journal of Advertising, 43*(1), 33–45.

Bamberg, S. (2003). How does environmental concern influence specific environmentally related behaviors? A new answer to an old question. *Journal of Environmental Psychology, 23*(1), 21–32.

Bayes, R., Bolsen, T., & Druckman, J. N. (2023). A research agenda for climate change communication and public opinion: The role of scientific consensus messaging and beyond. *Environmental Communication, 17*(1), 16–34.

Bhaskaran, S., Polonsky, M., Cary, J., & Fernandez, S. (2006). Environmentally sustainable food production and marketing: Opportunity or hype? *British Food Journal, 108*(8), 677–690.

Bronnmann, J., Asche, F., Pettersen, I. K., & Sogn-Grundvåg, G. (2023). Certify or not? The effect of the MSC certification on the ex-vessel prices for Atlantic cod in Norway. *Ecological Economics, 212,* 107940.

Blend, J. R., & Van Ravenswaay, E. O. (1999). Measuring consumer demand for ecolabeled apples. *American Journal of Agricultural Economics, 81*(5), 1072–1077.

Caswell, J. A., & Mojduszka, E. M. (1996). Using informational labeling to influence the market for quality in food products. *American Journal of Agricultural Economics, 78*(5), 1248–1253.

Connelly, B. L., Certo, S. T., Ireland, R. D., & Reutzel, C. R. (2011). Signaling theory: A review and assessment. *Journal of Management, 37*(1), 39–67.

Celsi, R. L., & Olson, J. C. (1988). The role of involvement in attention and comprehension processes. *Journal of Consumer Research, 15*(2), 210–224.

Clark, C. F., Kotchen, M. J., & Moore, M. R. (2003). Internal and external influences on pro-environmental behavior: Participation in a green electricity program. *Journal of Environmental Psychology, 23*(3), 237–246.

Dangelico, R. M., & Vocalelli, D. (2017). "Green Marketing": An analysis of definitions, strategy steps, and tools through a systematic review of the literature. *Journal of Cleaner Production, 165,* 1263–1279.

Darnall, N., Ji, H., & Vázquez-Brust, D. A. (2018). Third-party certification, sponsorship, and consumers' ecolabel use. *Journal of Business Ethics, 150,* 953–969.

de Graaff, V. C. (1996). *Private certification in a governance context: An assessment towards communicative governance.* Eburon.

Dekhili, S., & Achabou, M. A. (2014). Eco-labelling brand strategy: Independent certification versus self-declaration. *European Business Review, 26*(4), 305–329.

Delmas, M. A., & Lessem, N. (2017). Eco-premium or eco-penalty? Eco-labels and quality in the organic wine market. *Business & Society, 56*(2), 318–356.

Donato, C., & Adıgüzel, F. (2022). Visual complexity of eco-labels and product evaluations in online setting: Is simple always better? *Journal of Retailing and Consumer Services, 67,* 102961.

Donato, C., & D'Aniello, A. (2022). Tell me more and make me feel proud: The role of eco-labels and informational cues on consumers' food perceptions. *British Food Journal, 124*(4), 1365–1382.

D'Souza, C. (2004). Ecolabel programmes: A stakeholder (consumer) perspective. *Corporate Communications: An International Journal, 9*(3), 179–188.

Du, X. (2015). How the market values greenwashing? Evidence from China. *Journal of Business Ethics, 128,* 547–574.

Eldesouky, A., Mesias, F. J., & Escribano, M. (2020). Perception of Spanish consumers towards environmentally friendly labelling in food. *International Journal of Consumer Studies, 44*(1), 64–76.

Fazio, R. H. (1986). How do attitudes guide behavior. In *Handbook of motivation and cognition: Fountains of social behavior.* Lawrence Erlbaum Associates.

Grankvist, G., & Biel, A. (2001). The importance of beliefs and purchase criteria in the choice of eco-labeled food products. *Journal of Environmental Psychology, 21*(4), 405–410.

Grankvist, G., Lekedal, H., & Marmendal, M. (2007). Values and eco-and fair-trade labelled products. *British Food Journal, 109*(2), 169–181.

Grunert, K. G. (2013). Trends in food choice and nutrition. In *Consumer attitudes to food quality products: Emphasis on Southern Europe* (pp. 23–30).

Grunert, K. G., Hieke, S., & Wills, J. (2014). Sustainability labels on food products: Consumer motivation, understanding and use. *Food Policy, 44*, 177–189.

Gulbrandsen, L. H. (2006). Creating markets for eco-labelling: Are consumers insignificant? *International Journal of Consumer Studies, 30*(5), 477–489.

Hameed, I., & Waris, I. (2018). Eco labels and eco conscious consumer behavior: The mediating effect of green trust and environmental concern. *Journal of Management Sciences, 5*(2), 86–105.

Hemmelskamp, J., & Brockmann, K. L. (1997). Environmental labels—The German 'blue angel.' *Futures, 29*(1), 67–76.

Hopper, J. R., & Nielsen, J. M. (1991). Recycling as altruistic behavior: Normative and behavioral strategies to expand participation in a community recycling program. *Environment and Behavior, 23*(2), 195–220.

Horne, R. E. (2009). Limits to labels: The role of eco-labels in the assessment of product sustainability and routes to sustainable consumption. *International Journal of Consumer Studies, 33*(2), 175–182.

Johnston, R. J., Wessells, C. R., Donath, H., & Asche, F. (2001). Measuring consumer preferences for ecolabeled seafood: an international comparison. *Journal of Agricultural and resource Economics*, 20–39.

Karstens, B., & Belz, F. M. (2006). Information asymmetries, labels and trust in the German food market: A critical analysis based on the economics of information. *International Journal of Advertising, 25*(2), 189–211.

Kokkinaki, F. (1997). Involvement as a determinant of the process through which attitudes guide behavior. In *Proceedings from the IAREP XXII Conference* (pp. 52–67). Corpas, CB.

Lee, J. A., & Holden, S. J. (1999). Understanding the determinants of environmentally conscious behavior. *Psychology & Marketing, 16*(5), 373–392.

Loureiro, M. L., McCluskey, J. J., & Mittelhammer, R. C. (2001). Assessing consumer preferences for organic, eco-labeled, and regular apples. *Journal of Agricultural and Resource Economics*, 404–416.

Lotz, S., Christandl, F., & Fetchenhauer, D. (2013). What is fair is good: Evidence of consumers' taste for fairness. *Food Quality and Preference, 30*(2), 139–144.

Loureiro, M. L., & Lotade, J. (2005). Do fair trade and eco-labels in coffee wake up the consumer conscience? *Ecological Economics, 53*(1), 129–138.

Markandya, A. (1997). Eco-labelling: An introduction and review. *Eco-labelling and international trade* (pp. 1–20). Palgrave Macmillan UK.

McCluskey, J. J., & Loureiro, M. L. (2003). Consumer preferences and willingness to pay for food labeling: A discussion of empirical studies. *Journal of Food Distribution Research, 34*(3), 95–102.

Moon, W., Florkowski, W. J., Brückner, B., & Schonhof, I. (2002). Willingness to pay for environmental practices: Implications for eco-labeling. *Land Economics, 78*(1), 88–102.

Morris, J. (1997). *Green goods? Consumers, product labels and the environment.* IEA Environment Unit.

Nuttavuthisit, K., & Thøgersen, J. (2017). The importance of consumer trust for the emergence of a market for green products: The case of organic food. *Journal of Business Ethics, 140*, 323–337.

Ottman, J., & Books, N. B. (1998). Green marketing: Opportunity for innovation. *The Journal of Sustainable Product Design, 60*(7), 136–667.

Papadas, K. K., Avlonitis, G. J., & Carrigan, M. (2017). Green marketing orientation: Conceptualization, scale development and validation. *Journal of Business Research, 80*, 236–246.

Parguel, B., Benoit-Moreau, F., & Russell, C. A. (2015). Can evoking nature in advertising mislead consumers? The power of 'executive greenwashing.' *International Journal of Advertising, 34*(1), 107–134.

Park, C. W., & Young, S. M. (1986). Consumer response to television commercials: The impact of involvement and background music on brand attitude formation. *Journal of Marketing Research, 23*(1), 11–24.

Peattie, K. (1995). *Environmental marketing management: Meeting the green challenge* (pp. 705–726).

Peattie, K. (2001). Golden goose or wild goose? The hunt for the green consumer. *Business Strategy and the Environment, 10*(4), 187–199.

Pizzetti, M., Gatti, L., & Seele, P. (2021). Firms talk, suppliers walk: Analyzing the locus of greenwashing in the blame game and introducing 'vicarious greenwashing.' *Journal of Business Ethics, 170*(1), 21–38.

Pretty, J., & Ward, H. (2001). Social capital and the environment. *World Development, 29*(2), 209–227.

Prieto-Sandoval, V., Alfaro, J. A., Mejía-Villa, A., & Ormazabal, M. (2016). ECO-labels as a multidimensional research topic: Trends and opportunities. *Journal of Cleaner Production, 135*, 806–818.

Rao, A. R., Qu, L., & Ruekert, R. W. (1999). Signaling unobservable product quality through a brand ally. *Journal of Marketing Research, 36*(2), 258–268.

Rice, G. (2006). Pro-environmental behavior in Egypt: Is there a role for Islamic environmental ethics? *Journal of Business Ethics, 65,* 373–390.

Roberts, J. A. (1996). Green consumers in the 1990s: Profile and implications for advertising. *Journal of Business Research, 36*(3), 217–231.

Rousseau, S. (2015). The role of organic and fair trade labels when choosing chocolate. *Food Quality and Preference, 44,* 92–100.

Ruggeri, G., Corsi, S., & Nayga, R. M. (2021). Eliciting willingness to pay for fairtrade products with information. *Food Quality and Preference, 87,* 104066.

Sigurdsson, V., Larsen, N. M., Pálsdóttir, R. G., Folwarczny, M., Menon, R. V., & Fagerstrøm, A. (2022). Increasing the effectiveness of ecological food signaling: Comparing sustainability tags with eco-labels. *Journal of Business Research, 139,* 1099–1110.

Sirieix, L., Delanchy, M., Remaud, H., Zepeda, L., & Gurviez, P. (2013). Consumers' perceptions of individual and combined sustainable food labels: A UK pilot investigation. *International Journal of Consumer Studies, 37*(2), 143–151.

Sogn-Grundvåg, G., Larsen, T. A., & Young, J. A. (2013). The value of line-caught and other attributes: An exploration of price premiums for chilled fish in UK supermarkets. *Marine Policy, 38,* 41–44.

Sogn-Grundvåg, G., Larsen, T. A., & Young, J. A. (2014). Product differentiation with credence attributes and private labels: The case of whitefish in UK supermarkets. *Journal of Agricultural Economics, 65*(2), 368–382.

Sörqvist, P., Haga, A., Langeborg, L., Holmgren, M., Wallinder, M., Nöstl, A., Seager, P. B., & Marsh, J. E. (2015). The green halo: Mechanisms and limits of the eco-label effect. *Food Quality and Preference, 43,* 1–9.

Sörqvist, P., Hedblom, D., Holmgren, M., Haga, A., Langeborg, L., Nöstl, A., & Kågström, J. (2013). Who needs cream and sugar when there is eco-labeling? Taste and willingness to pay for "eco-friendly" coffee. *PLoS ONE, 8*(12), e80719.

Stern, P. C. (1999). Information, incentives, and proenvironmental consumer behavior. *Journal of Consumer Policy, 22*(4), 461–478.

Stern, P. C. (2005). Understanding individuals' environmentally significant behavior. *Environmental Law Reporter News & Analysis, 35,* 10785.

Straughan, R. D., & Roberts, J. A. (1999). Environmental segmentation alternatives: A look at green consumer behavior in the new millennium. *Journal of Consumer Marketing, 16*(6), 558–575.

Teisl, M. F. (2003). What we may have is a failure to communicate*: Labeling environmentally certified forest products. *Forest Science, 49*(5), 668–680.

Teisl, M. F., & Roe, B. (2005). Evaluating the factors that impact the effectiveness of eco-labelling programmes. In *Environment, information and consumer behaviour* (pp. 65–90).

Testa, F., Iraldo, F., Vaccari, A., & Ferrari, E. (2015). Why eco-labels can be effective marketing tools: Evidence from a study on Italian consumers. *Business Strategy and the Environment, 24*(4), 252–265.

Thøgersen, J. (1999). The ethical consumer. Moral norms and packaging choice. *Journal of Consumer Policy, 22*, 439–460.

Thøgersen, J. (2000). Psychological determinants of paying attention to eco-labels in purchase decisions: Model development and multinational validation. *Journal of Consumer Policy, 23*(3), 285–313.

Thøgersen, J. (2002). Promoting green consumer behavior with eco-labels. In *New tools for environmental protection* (pp. 83–104).

Thøgersen, J. (2010). Country differences in sustainable consumption: The case of organic food. *Journal of Macromarketing, 30*(2), 171–185.

Thøgersen, J., Haugaard, P., & Olesen, A. (2010). Consumer responses to ecolabels. *European Journal of Marketing, 44*(11/12), 1787–1810.

Thorson, E., Page, T., & Moore, J. (1995). Consumer response to four categories of "Green" television commercials. *Advances in Consumer Research, 22*(1).

Van Amstel, M., Driessen, P., & Glasbergen, P. (2008). Eco-labeling and information asymmetry: A comparison of five eco-labels in the Netherlands. *Journal of Cleaner Production, 16*(3), 263–276.

Wiedmann, K. P., Hennigs, N., Henrik Behrens, S., & Klarmann, C. (2014). Tasting green: An experimental design for investigating consumer perception of organic wine. *British Food Journal, 116*(2), 197–211.

Zarrilli, S., Jha, V., & Vossenaar, R. (Eds.). (1997). *Eco-labelling and international trade*. Macmillan.

Zelezny, L. C., Chua, P. P., & Aldrich, C. (2000). New ways of thinking about environmentalism: Elaborating on gender differences in environmentalism. *Journal of Social Issues, 56*(3), 443–457.

CHAPTER 3

Aesthetic Influence on Consumer Behavior

Abstract This chapter defines the concept of aesthetics and its influence on consumer behavior, emphasizing its impact on visual appeal and the evaluation of visual stimuli. It discusses aesthetic psychology and the dimensions of aesthetic experience, highlighting the roles of psychographic and collative variables in appreciating visual stimuli. The chapter delves into the fluency process as a key mechanism that explains the relationships between visual dimensions and aesthetic appreciation. Additionally, it examines how aesthetic dimensions and fluency affect consumer perceptions across various marketing domains, including eco-labels, showcasing their importance in shaping consumer attitudes and decision-making processes.

Keywords Aesthetics · Psychophysical variables · Collative variables · Fluency theory · Eco-label design

1 INTRODUCTION

The aim of this chapter is to clarify what is meant by aesthetics to gain a deeper understanding of how this concept can significantly influence consumer behavior. Aesthetics encompasses much more than mere visual appeal; it involves the intricate ways in which individuals interpret and

© The Author(s), under exclusive license to Springer Nature Switzerland AG 2025
C. Donato, *Eco-Label Visual Design and Sustainability*,
https://doi.org/10.1007/978-3-031-82761-7_3

respond to their surroundings. This chapter specifically seeks to explore the pivotal role of aesthetics in the evaluation of products and graphic stimuli, shedding light on how aesthetic perceptions shape consumer experiences and choices.

Traditionally, the importance of aesthetics was often confined to discussions of physical appearance or the realm of art. However, in a contemporary commercial context, this importance has expanded to include not only products but also any other elements that represent a company, such as product packaging, brand identity, and logos. In today's competitive markets, the aesthetic appeal of these elements can be a decisive factor influencing consumer preferences and loyalty.

In the first section, an attempt is made to define "aesthetic experience." Following this, the focus will shift to the various aesthetic dimensions, particularly referencing the influential studies conducted by Berlyne, whose work highlights how factors such as complexity, novelty, and ambiguity can impact aesthetic appreciation. Additionally, a brief examination of the concepts of proportion and balance will be provided, emphasizing their significance in creating aesthetically pleasing compositions that resonate with viewers.

The subsequent sections will highlight ongoing research in the area of fluency, which is a key area of inquiry aimed at elucidating the cognitive processes involved in perceiving aesthetic dimensions. This body of research aims to unpack how fluency—the ease with which information is processed—can affect individuals' judgments of beauty and aesthetic value. Understanding these processes provides valuable insights into the complex interplay between aesthetics and human perception, ultimately contributing to a more comprehensive understanding of how aesthetics shape experiences and behaviors.

This examination of aesthetic dimensions and fluency will ultimately reveal how these factors influence consumer behavior, shaping not only preferences and decision-making processes but also fostering deeper emotional connections between consumers and various marketing domains, including product, retail, advertising, brand, and logo design.

2   AESTHETIC PSYCHOLOGY
AND THE DIMENSIONS OF AESTHETIC EXPERIENCE

Aesthetics is a complex science that emerged from the combination of various disciplines: sociology, aesthetics, psychology, mathematics, anthropology, psychoanalysis, and art theory. This discipline was "officially" established in 1750 with the publication of the book "*Aesthetica*" by Alexander Gottlieb Baumgarten, who understood it as "*the science of beauty, the liberal arts, and lower gnoseology, sister of logic*" (Mirbach, 2009).

Aesthetic experiences, a concept rooted in the artistic domain, have now permeated various sectors, including marketing, design, and user experience. An aesthetic experience refers to the subjective emotional response individuals have when engaging with an object or environment they find aesthetically pleasing or meaningful. As explored by Silvia (2012) and Freeman (2010), such experiences generate pleasure through the transformative power of beauty. One of the most significant contributions to the understanding of aesthetics comes from Berlyne (1971), who is widely regarded as the true founder of Aesthetic Psychology, the study of individuals' reactions to beauty and art.

Based on various experimental studies (Berlyne, 1966), it can be established that the properties of stimuli that seemingly govern aesthetic appreciation consist essentially of those that determine the so-called "*arousal potential*," or the degree of stimulation a visual stimulus can potentially elicit in the observer. In turn, arousal indicators can be influenced by the *psychophysical variables* present in a stimulus, such as intensity (Berlyne, 1961), color (e.g., Ball, 1965; Wilson, 1966), and size (e.g., Silvera et al., 2002), and by the *collative variables*, such as the degree of novelty (e.g., Berlyne et al., 1963); uncertainty (Berlyne & Borsa, 1968); and complexity (Baker & Franken, 1967; Berlyne & McDonnell, 1965; Berlyne et al., 1963; Bryson & Driver, 1972; Gibson et al., 1967).

Additionally, the concepts of proportion and balance, although not directly classified under the aforementioned categories, are also key elements in identifying preferences and affective states a subject may experience when confronted with a specific visual stimulus.

2.1   Psychophysical Variables

Psychophysical variables include characteristics that directly impact visual perception and enable an initial evaluation of a stimulus's pleasantness (Martindale & Moore, 1989). These variables encompass the intensity of the visual stimulus, referring to the degree of energy and power it evokes (Guilford, 1934); its size, which pertains to dimensions such as length and width (Martin, 1906); and its color, which refers to the perceptual experience of different wavelengths of light as interpreted by the human brain (Berlyne, 1971).

2.1.1   Intensity

Intensity plays an important role in visual perception. This variable refers to the strength or vividness of an aesthetic experience elicited by visual elements. High-intensity visual stimuli are characterized by bright colors, high contrast, or dynamic forms (Berlyne, 1971). This intensity can influence aesthetic appreciation and consumer preferences, as more intense visuals often capture attention and evoke stronger feelings (Palmer & Schloss, 2010). In an experiment conducted by Guilford (1934) using colored squares placed on a gray background, it was found that more intense (i.e., vivid) shades were perceived as more pleasant compared to duller ones. However, the intensity of a color patch is influenced by the incidence of light; when the colored squares are placed in front of a light source (e.g., a window), the perceived intensity, along with pleasantness, increases up to a certain maximum point. Beyond this threshold, any further increase in brightness results in a decline in perceived pleasantness (Fig. 1).

When examining the curve of pleasantness for shades lacking chromatic effects, such as white, gray, and black, an interesting pattern emerges. Figures that lean toward white are judged as more pleasant than those in black or gray, while brighter forms appear to fall around a point of indifference.

2.1.2   Size

The term "size" refers to the overall dimensions of a graphic representation, including both length and width. Preferences for larger images may have different implications compared to preferences for smaller ones, potentially reflecting varying degrees of egocentrism or a desire for prominence (Amatulli et al., 2020). In an experiment conducted by Martin

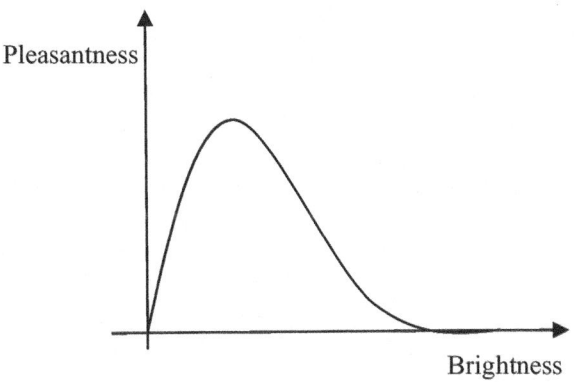

Fig. 1 Relationship between pleasantness and brightness (*Source* Guilford, 1934)

(1906), participants were presented with 26 circles, ranging from 1 to 500 mm in diameter, and asked to express their preferences. The results showed indifference toward smaller circles, but "beyond a certain size," preferences increased as the diameter grew, up to a point, after which preference began to decline. Emotional responses to larger stimuli also tend to be stronger due to their higher arousal potential. These findings align with the Wundt curve (see Fig. 2), which suggests that moderate levels of arousal are perceived as more pleasant, while excessively large stimuli can lead to discomfort or negative reactions (Berlyne, 1971).

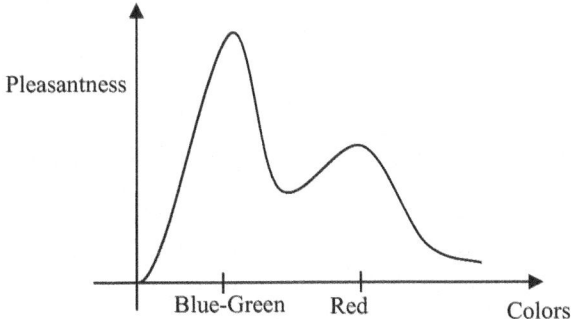

Fig. 2 Relationship between pleasantness and colors (*Source* Guilford, 1940)

2.1.3   Color

Color, as a psychophysical dimension, refers to the perception of light wavelengths reflected from surfaces, resulting in different hues, brightness, and saturation. Hue refers to the type of color (e.g., red or blue), saturation indicates the level or purity of the color, and brightness reflects the perceived lightness or darkness. These factors combine to create the complex perception of color, which is shaped by both the physical properties of light (such as wavelength) and the psychological processes involved in interpreting them (Fairchild, 2013).

Color considerably influences aesthetic experience, with research showing that bright colors are often perceived as more pleasant and stimulating compared to duller hues (Guilford, 1934). In particular, Guilford (1940) conducted an experiment under rigorously controlled conditions, where the various colors were separated based on hue, brightness, and purity, in order to test sample preferences. The author confirmed that the curve describing the relationship between pleasantness and various color tones has two peaks: a primary one around the green–blue area and a secondary one around the red (Fig. 2).

According to Berlyne (1971), colors with moderate levels of arousal potential are most aesthetically pleasing, while extremely intense or highly contrasting colors can lead to overstimulation or discomfort. Furthermore, the ability of colors to harmonize with one another plays a critical role in enhancing aesthetic appeal. Helson and Landford (1970) conducted additional experiments, demonstrating an inverse relationship between color concentration and perceived harmony, with optimal harmony occurring at equal brightness levels. Their findings underscored the importance of brightness contrast between colors and backgrounds in determining pleasantness and harmony.

2.2   Collative Variables

Collative variables are essential concepts in aesthetic psychology, referring to the features of stimuli that can enhance or diminish their aesthetic appeal. These variables include novelty, uncertainty, and complexity, which influence emotional responses and cognitive engagement. Novelty refers to the degree of newness or unfamiliarity of a stimulus (Hekkert & Wieringen, 1996). Uncertainty refers to the degree to which an individual cannot predict the outcome of an event or the nature of a stimulus, leading to increased cognitive engagement and exploration contributing to aesthetic pleasure (Morreall, 1983). Complexity pertains to the richness of details within a stimulus (Berlyne, 1971). Together, these variables shape how individuals perceive and appreciate art, design, and other forms of creative expression, highlighting the interplay between cognitive processing and emotional engagement in aesthetic experiences (Marin, 2022).

The following paragraphs will delve into each collative variable in detail, examining previous studies and their implications in terms of perception, aesthetic preferences, and cognitive responses.

2.2.1   Novelty

Novelty is a critical collative variable in aesthetic psychology, defined as the amount of variety and diversity in a stimulus pattern (Berlyne, 1960).

Research indicates that novel stimuli tend to capture attention and evoke positive emotions, while familiar stimuli may elicit indifference or reduced interest (Hekkert & Wieringen, 1996). An early and pivotal attempt to identify the determinants of novelty was conducted by Berlyne and Parham (1968), who presented irregular shapes to subjects for nine seconds and then asked them to evaluate each stimulus on a seven-point scale, ranging from "very familiar" to "very unfamiliar." Their findings revealed three important insights: first, the perceived novelty of a stimulus decreases with repeated exposure; second, the degree of novelty diminishes when a stimulus resembles previously presented stimuli; and third, a stimulus is considered "new" to the extent that it differs from others seen before. These conclusions underscore the dynamic nature of novelty in aesthetic experiences and highlight how exposure and similarity can shape perception.

Further experiments by Berlyne (1961) demonstrated the impact of novelty on exploratory behavior. In this study, pairs of figures representing animals were projected for ten seconds, during which subjects could see both new and previously shown figures side by side. Results indicated that participants spent significantly more time looking at figures they encountered for the first time compared to those they had already seen, reinforcing the notion that novelty drives attention and interest. Many researchers (Day, 1966; Haywood & Hunt, 1963; Leckart, 1966) have also observed a certain decrease in looking time when a multitude of figures is presented in succession. In other words, excessive exposure to a variety of stimuli with a certain degree of originality, and therefore differentiation, tends to diminish the motivational effect of novelty. Psycho-physiological experiments (Berlyne et al., 1963) have indeed confirmed that a succession of new stimuli over time becomes progressively less capable of reviving and invigorating individual reactions, which tend to weaken.

Considering the case of presenting a single stimulus, some experiments have verified that the perceived degree of novelty in a certain image tends to decrease progressively if the image is presented multiple times over time, thus influencing both judgments of pleasantness and preference (Berlyne, 1970). However, some experiments by Zajonc (1968) seem to have precisely opposite implications, suggesting that familiar stimuli are more likely to receive a positive evaluation than new stimuli. Zajonc (1968) used Chinese characters and nonsensical Turkish words, asking participants to assign meanings to them. Words closer to a common language were rated more positively, while those more foreign and rich in novelty were viewed negatively. This contradiction highlights the complex interplay between novelty and other factors such as familiarity, complexity, and context.

The relationship between novelty and complexity has been extensively studied, particularly in Berlyne's (1970) work. In one experiment, participants rated the pleasantness of black-and-white reproductions of complex and simple figures. Initially, both complex and simple patterns received similar ratings, but after ten repetitions, complex patterns were rated more favorably, while simpler ones lost their appeal. These findings align with the Wundt curve (see Fig. 3), which relates the degree of arousal generated by a stimulus to its hedonic value. The Wundt curve illustrates the relationship between the arousal a stimulus generates and its hedonic value. A highly complex stimulus, when presented for the first time, tends to evoke maximum novelty and arousal (area C of the curve). However, as exposure is repeated, the perceived novelty—and consequently the arousal—diminishes (area B). Initially, a completely new stimulus may not be judged as very pleasant (area C), but with repeated exposure and reduced novelty, its pleasantness can increase, reaching a peak (part B), before eventually declining again as the stimulus becomes familiar or even uninteresting.

In contrast, for extremely simple and familiar stimuli, both the level of arousal and hedonic value remain low (part A of the curve).

Then, according to this model, a highly novel stimulus initially generates maximum arousal but becomes less exciting with repeated exposure,

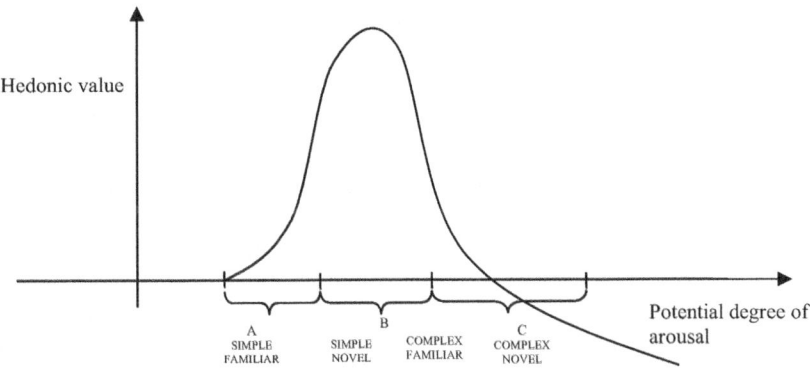

Fig. 3   The Wundt curve in relation to stimulus complexity

while pleasantness increases, peaks, and then declines as novelty fades—similar to trends in music or fashion.

Berlyne (1970) demonstrated this in an experiment where subjects rated two simple and two complex images. Each image was viewed eight times, and as expected, the pleasantness ratings for complex stimuli increased, peaking during the third exposure before declining. In contrast, ratings for simple stimuli steadily declined, with only a slight recovery at the end.

This evidence highlights how familiarity affects stimulus perception: repeated exposure to complex stimuli generally increases their perceived hedonic value, whereas the opposite occurs with simple stimuli.

2.2.2   Uncertainty

In the realm of aesthetics, uncertainty emerges when a stimulus is ambiguous or unpredictable, prompting increased attention and cognitive engagement as individuals seek to resolve this ambiguity (Berlyne, 1971). Berlyne (1958) demonstrated that ambiguous figures containing incongruous elements (such as an animal with an elephant's body and a bird's head) captured human attention for longer durations than images that accurately depicted reality. This observation was further supported by Nunnally et al. (1969), who monitored subjects' eye movements and found that the more irrational the presented figure, the longer the subjects focused on it. Eye movement studies have shown that the gaze tends to focus on areas with high informational content, unusual details, and elements that clarify the nature of the depicted scene (Mackworth & Bruner, 1966; Mackworth & Morandi, 1967; Yarbus, 2013). Further research highlights the role of uncertainty in shaping both aesthetic experiences and consumer behavior. For example, Berger and Milkman (2012) found that emotionally charged content—especially shocking—has a higher likelihood of being shared, driven by heightened emotional arousal, a key factor in both aesthetic evaluation and decision-making.

In conclusion, uncertainty functions as a force in aesthetics and consumer responses, fostering pleasure and engagement when well-applied, but risking disorientation or discomfort if misused. This collative variable is crucial in design and marketing, influencing how consumers interpret and emotionally react to both creative and commercial stimuli.

2.2.3   Complexity

Complexity refers to the degree to which an artifact, such as visual content, is composed of multiple distinct elements that interact in various ways to create an emergent experience greater than the sum of its parts (Anderson, 1972). Berlyne (1960) identified several critical properties defining complexity: it increases with the number and dissimilarity of elements, while it decreases when those elements can be perceived as a cohesive unit.

Several experimental studies have sought to elucidate the variables encompassed by this variable. Research by Berlyne et al. (1968) showed that subjective complexity is strongly influenced by the informational content of figures. As the number of elements and their combinations increased, the perceived complexity also rose.

Munsinger and Kessen (1964) employed scales to measure the pleasantness of polygons ranging from three to 40 sides. Their experiments revealed that shapes with three and ten sides were rated as the most pleasant. Later studies confirmed that individuals tended to find more complex images increasingly enjoyable.

Day (1967) found that perceived complexity increased with the number of sides, with symmetric polygons rated as less complex than asymmetric ones when they had the same number of sides. This relationship is well established: complexity is directly proportional to the number of elements and inversely related to their redundancy (Houston et al., 1965; Karmel, 1969). Specifically, perceived complexity tends to diminish as redundancy increases in the stimuli presented (Mindus, 1968). Furthermore, polygons that are novel or previously unseen are judged to be more complex and possess a higher novelty factor (Eisenman, 1969) than familiar ones. This suggests a nuanced interplay between novelty and complexity, with the former affecting short-term perception and the latter influenced by long-term familiarity and perceptual organization processes.

Moreover, Hoats et al. (1963) firstly and Berlyne (1971) later showed that subjects preferred complex images, driven by curiosity and the uncertainty these images evoked. Studies by Berlyne and Crozier (1971) linked these preferences to arousal potential and information processing. In low-stimulation environments, individuals often seek complex stimuli to avoid boredom. For instance, Jones et al., (1961) noted that sensory deprivation leads to a desire for unpredictable stimuli, while Leckart et al. (1970) showed that brief low-arousal conditions increased the preference for complex shapes, with longer deprivation enhancing the desire for visual complexity.

To encapsulate aesthetic appeal, many scholars have employed terms such as "uniformity in variety," referring to the combination of elements with both similarities and differences. In a series of experiments by Berlyne and Boudewijns (1971), visual images composed of two elements, differing in up to four characteristics, revealed that perceived pleasantness is inversely correlated with the number of differences, while direct relationships existed between differences and interest.

The distinction between pleasantness and interest is crucial, as they represent different experiences. Interest involves attention and engagement with an object, while pleasantness refers to the enjoyment derived from it. Research suggests that very simple visual stimuli, which Gestalt theory (i.e., the idea that individuals perceive whole forms or patterns rather than just the sum of their parts, Koffka, 2013) might classify as "*prägnant*," can be pleasant but lack interest. In contrast, stimuli that are both pleasant and interesting tend to have more complexity and internal order. Complex images often evoke curiosity and mild disorientation, inviting deeper engagement, while simple patterns may increase hedonic value but fail to provoke sustained interest.

As familiarity with complex stimuli grows, interest and perceived complexity initially rise before declining, while pleasantness increases but eventually drops off. Berlyne and Lewis (1963) found that, after repeated exposure to image pairs, subjects often favored less complex images, aligning with earlier studies that rated them as more pleasant.

Overall, this body of research highlights how visual complexity plays a pivotal role in shaping aesthetic experiences, driving both initial curiosity and sustained engagement with stimuli through its interaction with novelty and familiarity.

2.3   Proportion and Balance

This paragraph addresses two critical elements in aesthetic psychology and visual design—proportion and the balance that images can evoke in observers—even though they are not explicitly mentioned in the categorization of psychographic and collative variables. Proportion refers to the harmonious relationship between elements, focusing on their size and spatial arrangement relative to one another (Huntley, 2012). Balance is the visual distribution of elements in a composition, ensuring that no part overwhelms the others. It can be *symmetrical* (evenly distributed) or *asymmetrical* (differently arranged but visually stable), contributing to visual equilibrium and harmony in design (Lidwell et al., 2010).

The importance of proportions in aesthetic has been analyzed by mathematicians since the time of the ancient Greeks, with Pythagoras being the first to highlight, in the sixth century B.C. The Pythagorean tradition, in turn, was one of the main inspirations for Aristotle and Plato, who vacillated between the conviction that art should represent a perfect imitation of reality and the more formalistic viewpoint that emphasized the relationship between the depicted elements and their quantitative accuracy. Plato (in the *Philebus*) wrote that *"in all things, measure and proportion constitute beauty and virtue"*; Aristotle (in the *Metaphysics*) listed order (*taxis*), completeness (*horismenon*), and quantitative appropriateness (*symmetria*) as the mathematical foundations of beauty (Berlyne, 1971).

Throughout history, the relationship between proportions and aesthetic satisfaction has been explored in numerous treatises, most notably by Vitruvius in the first century B.C. and Dürer in the sixth century, both focusing on human portraiture. A particular ratio has emerged as especially significant: the *golden ratio*, defined mathematically as $\frac{A}{B} = \frac{B}{(A+B)}$, where A represents the shorter length and B the longer length. This relationship yields a value of approximately φ (1.618), known variously as the "divine proportion," or "golden section," reflecting its enduring appeal and importance in art and architecture (see Berlyne, 1971).

In the nineteenth century, Zeising (1855) identified the golden section as essential to beauty in visual arts, characterizing it as the foundation of "proportionality" and a superior form of "pure beauty" achieved through symmetry and similarity among components. Empirical studies (Eysenck & Tunstall, 1968; Lalo, 1908; Thorndike, 1917; Witmer, 1894) confirmed a preference for shapes that approximate the golden section, indicating a general liking for proportionality and symmetry in design (Day, 1968).

However, balance and symmetry can often lead to excessive similarity, creating a sense of monotony.

What viewers often seek is balance where distinct yet equivalent subunits are arranged near a central focus (Berlyne, 1971). Balance, symmetry, and equivalence are critical formal elements in both visual and temporal arts; for instance, dramatic compositions require a balance between recent and earlier episodes.

Pierce (1895) was among the first to investigate these concepts experimentally, using an image with a central vertical line and adjusting figures until subjects deemed the composition "balanced." Puffer (1903) refined this approach by allowing subjects to move elements themselves, focusing on achieving a "pleasant" rather than strictly "balanced" image. Results indicated that smaller elements were often placed farther from larger ones, with colored images gravitating toward the center compared to black-and-white images.

These findings suggest that the characteristics of aesthetically balanced images relate closely to arousal and attention, with stimuli placed near the center more likely to draw focus.

In summary, the interplay of proportion and balance in visual design not only shapes aesthetic appreciation but also influences viewers' engagement and emotional responses to imagery.

3 UNRAVELING FLUENCY: COGNITIVE MECHANISMS BEHIND AESTHETIC JUDGMENTS

Having established how aesthetic dimensions affect attention and arousal, it becomes essential to delve into the cognitive processes that mediate these responses, particularly those linked to fluency defined as the ease with which information is processed by individuals, influencing their aesthetic and cognitive evaluations of stimuli (Reber et al., 1998).

What is beauty? This question has been debated for over 2,500 years, generating a wide range of responses (Feagin, 1995). Two major perspectives stand out:

- The *objective theory*, supported by theorists like Plato, defines beauty, or aesthetic appreciation, as an intrinsic quality of an object that elicits a pleasant experience in the observer (Tatarkiewicz, 1970). This approach has led psychologists to identify key factors that define beauty, including balance and proportion (Arnheim, 1943; Gombrich, 2023), symmetry (Arnheim, 1943; Gombrich, 2023; Humphrey, 1997), informational content and complexity (Berlyne, 1971, 1974; Eysenck, 1941; Garner, 2014), as well as contrast and brightness (Gombrich, 2023; Solso, 1994).
- The *subjective theory*, on the other hand, argues that anything can be beautiful if it pleases the senses (Tatarkiewicz, 1970). According to this view, beauty depends on the observer's personal traits, making any search for universal laws of beauty futile. This viewpoint is summarized by the well-known expressions "*beauty is in the eye of the beholder*" and "*de gustibus non est disputandum*" (i.e., there's no disputing taste).

However, some philosophical analyses tend to reject this rigid distinction. Instead, they propose that aesthetic appreciation emerges from the relationship between people and objects (Ingarden & McCormick, 1985; Murray, 1989). The pleasantness of an image, therefore, stems from a subject's experience, shaped by the interaction between the properties of the stimulus and the subject's cognitive and emotional processes.

In this context, although judgments of acceptability or preference for a visual stimulus may involve different processes, research on the "mere exposure" effect has highlighted the fluency model as a compelling theoretical explanation for these relationships. The fluency model suggests that prior exposure to a stimulus facilitates its perception, encoding, and processing when encountered again (Bornstein & D'Agostino, 1992, 1994).

Assuming that repeated exposure increases perceived fluency, numerous studies have sought to identify the conditions under which fluency arises (Jost et al., 2013). However, less attention has been given to understanding the source of this fluency. Initially, Berlyne's two-factor theory (1970) proposed that fluency from repeated exposure is a byproduct of learning. Later, experiments by Janiszewski and Meyvis (2001) supported the dual-process theory (Groves & Thompson, 1970), which suggests that fluency results from the subject's response to the perceptual characteristics of the stimulus, generating both "sensitization" and "habituation" in the neural system.

Processing a stimulus involves a variety of internal mental processes that do not always relate directly to the content of the stimulus. For instance, mental processes involved in perceiving the same stimulus can differ in their activation levels (Mandler et al., 1987), speed (Jacoby, 1983), or the effort required (Schwarz, 2013). While these parameters vary, they are often broadly grouped under the term fluency (Kelley & Jacoby, 1990; Schwarz, 2013). It is generally believed that individuals can access this fluency through metacognitive feedback mechanisms (Mazzoni & Nelson, 1995; Metcalf & Shimamura, 1994). These mechanisms may make fluency available for other cognitive processes, including affective responses. Interestingly, the fluency signal may not always require the simultaneous presence of the stimulus content and can even emerge unconsciously, sometimes preceding conscious awareness of the stimulus (Seamon et al., 1983).

Setting aside these initial observations, it is useful to make some distinctions. *Objective fluency* refers to a mental process characterized by objective judgments—marked by high speed, precision, and minimal effort. In contrast, *subjective fluency* refers to the individual's conscious experience of easy processing, which requires low cognitive effort and is shaped by the person's specific characteristics (Alter & Oppenheimer, 2009).

Another important distinction is between *perceptual fluency* and *conceptual fluency* (Reber et al., 1998; Whittlesea, 1993). Perceptual fluency reflects the ease of processing a stimulus based on its surface characteristics or perceptual form. It is influenced by factors such as the duration of exposure or repeated presentations of the stimulus, even in the form of priming. For example, to make an image more familiar to an observer, it can be shown in an initial sequence alongside other control stimuli and then reintroduced later. Studies show that such manipulations can immediately affect subjects' responses by altering the speed and accuracy of perceptual identification (Jacoby, 1983; Roediger, 1990; Tulving & Schachter, 1990).

On the other hand, conceptual fluency refers to the ease of processing a stimulus at a higher level, facilitating operations such as categorization, and understanding the relationship between the stimulus and its semantic meaning. Conceptual fluency is affected by factors such as semantic priming (i.e., priming related to a stimulus's content and meaning), semantic predictability, and contextual congruence (Kelley & Jacoby, 1998; McGlone & Tofighbakhsh, 2000; Roediger, 1990; Whittlesea, 1993).

While perceptual and conceptual fluency are distinct processes, they may support each other when stimulus information is "poor" (i.e., fragmented, degraded, or ambiguous), often leading to similar judgments. Consequently, these processes are often summarized under the broader term *fluency*. Notably, stimuli are generally evaluated more positively when associated with a high level of fluency, implying that fluency has a hedonic quality. A high level of fluency typically signals positivity within the environment or the cognitive system, while a low level of fluency signals negativity.

The underlying reason for this phenomenon remains a topic of exploration. One primary explanation is that high fluency generates positive affective states because it suggests the stimulus is familiar to the observer or has been encountered before. This link between fluency and familiarity is supported by various empirical studies. First, familiar stimuli are processed more quickly than novel ones (Haber & Hershenson, 1965; Jacoby & Dallas, 1981). Second, familiar stimuli require less attention than new stimuli, thus reducing cognitive effort (Desimone et al., 1995). Third, familiar stimuli prompt faster, more refined, and more consistent cognitive and behavioral responses than unfamiliar ones (Lewenstein & Nowak, 1989; Norman et al., 2000). These effects can arise at any stage of stimulus processing, often without the need to recognize specific features of the stimulus. However, the question remains as to why familiarity has such a positive valence. Research suggests that this connection stems from a biological predisposition to approach familiar stimuli with caution, as unfamiliar stimuli may signal potential danger (Zajonc, 1968). This instinctive "fear of the unknown" has been observed across various animal species in response to different stimuli.

Another key observation is that symmetrical and prototypical stimuli are processed more quickly and easily, resulting in positive affective states (Checkosky & Whitlock, 1973; Palmer, 1991; Posner & Keele, 1968). People generally prefer such forms; for instance, symmetrical faces are typically favored over asymmetrical ones (Berlyne, 1970). Similarly, there is a noted preference for prototypical forms, which are representative of the category they belong to, indicating a degree of familiarity. As previously mentioned, familiarity fosters positive emotional responses.

In summary, high levels of fluency typically generate positive affective states, while low levels of fluency tend to evoke negative ones. A stimulus can be processed fluently either because of prior exposure or due to its inherent characteristics.

The following sections will delve deeper into fluency processes, distinguishing between two primary forms: perceptual fluency and conceptual fluency, and their roles in influencing consumers' responses.

3.1   Perceptual Fluency

Perceptual fluency refers to the ease with which a stimulus is processed based on its perceptual or visual characteristics, such as its clarity, symmetry, or simplicity (Bornstein & D'Agostino, 1994; Janiszewski, 1988, 1990, 1993; Shapiro, 1999). This concept has garnered attention in cognitive psychology, particularly for its role in shaping individuals' affective responses to stimuli. Interest in the link between perceptual fluency and individuals' evaluations largely stems from research on the "mere exposure" effect (Zajonc, 1968), which argues that repeated exposure to a stimulus over time leads to increased liking. Essentially, the more often people are exposed to a particular stimulus, the more pleasing it becomes, as familiarity allows for easier processing. Over the years, several studies have established a strong relationship between this effect and perceptual fluency (Bornstein & D'Agostino, 1994; Klinger & Greenwald, 1994; Seamon et al., 1983), suggesting that the ease with which a stimulus is processed plays a critical role in how it is judged.

Repeated exposure to a stimulus not only accelerates identification but also enhances judgments regarding clarity and content, independent of the actual exposure duration (Jacoby & Dallas, 1981; Whittlesea et al., 1990; Witherspoon & Allan, 1985). Essentially, the more fluently a stimulus is processed, the more positive evaluations it tends to receive. This correlation between perceptual fluency and positive affect has been observed across various domains, from simple shapes to complex social stimuli, making it a crucial concept in understanding aesthetic preferences. Even after a single exposure, stimuli that are processed with greater ease tend to be evaluated more favorably. This suggests that fluency plays a significant role not just in repeated encounters but in first impressions as well, marking it as a central mechanism in shaping individuals' aesthetic and emotional judgments.

To test the link between perceptual fluency and preference, Reber et al. (1998) conducted several experiments. In one, 53 participants evaluated 20 images of neutral objects (e.g., horses, airplanes) presented for two seconds each. Recognition was challenged by distorting the foreground by 30% and the background by 40%. A highly distorted version of the same object was then flashed briefly as a prime. Participants rated each object's attractiveness on a scale from 1 to 9. The results showed that images preceded by matching primes were recognized faster and rated more positively, highlighting how perceptual fluency influences judgments.

In another experiment, visual contrast between the foreground and background of a series of circles was manipulated. Participants consistently preferred high-contrast figures, which were easier to process, reinforcing the link between perceptual fluency and positive affect. This suggests that stimuli processed more easily tend to elicit more favorable emotional responses, even without deep cognitive engagement.

To further confirm that perceptual fluency, rather than inherent properties of the stimuli, drove preferences, a third experiment varied presentation time while keeping visual contrast constant. Longer exposure allowed participants to extract more information from each stimulus, enhancing perceptual fluency through easier processing. As expected, stimuli presented for longer durations received more favorable ratings, confirming that increased perceptual fluency leads to more positive evaluations.

The study also aimed to clarify whether fluency solely generates positive affect or can elicit neutral responses. Participants rated stimuli based on "liking" and "disliking," revealing that high fluency consistently resulted in positive affect rather than neutral or negative reactions.

A subsequent experiment examined the link between perceptual fluency and affective judgments by varying exposure duration. Results confirmed previous findings: longer presentation times increased perceptual fluency and pleasantness ratings, while stimuli processed with difficulty were rated as more unpleasant. These results further underscore the strong connection between perceptual fluency and positive affect, emphasizing the importance of processing ease in shaping emotional responses.

This body of research highlights the nature of affective responses elicited by perceptual fluency. Winkielman and Cacioppo (2001) explored this using facial electromyography (EMG), which detects subtle muscle movements tied to emotional expressions. Positive affective responses are linked to increased zygomatic muscle activity (the "smiling" muscles), while negative affect correlates with heightened activity in the frontal muscles (the "frowning" muscles), such as furrowing the eyebrows (Cacioppo et al., 1986; Lang et al., 1993). In their study, participants viewed images of several objects and rated the emotional responses elicited by these images. Results showed that high fluency correlated with increased zygomatic activity, indicating positive affect, while no increase in frowning activity was observed, confirming that fluency primarily generates positive emotions. Importantly, these affective responses emerged within the first three seconds of stimulus presentation, before participants consciously evaluated the images. This finding underscores that fluency triggers spontaneous affective responses prior to conscious judgment, highlighting the emotional impact of processing ease.

Overall, these studies demonstrate that perceptual fluency significantly influences individuals' affective responses to stimuli. Whether through repeated exposure, visual priming, or extended presentation times, stimuli that are processed more fluently receive higher ratings and elicit positive emotional states. The ease of processing signals safety, familiarity, and pleasantness, reinforcing fluency's fundamental role in shaping human preferences and aesthetic judgments.

3.2   Conceptual Fluency

Thus far, the discussion has primarily focused on the consequences of perceptual fluency, but it is essential to recognize that fluency is not confined to perceptual aspects alone. Parallel effects can be observed in what is known as conceptual fluency. Tversky and Kahneman (1973) indicate that individuals often base judgments on "the ease with which examples or associations come to mind." Therefore, a stimulus that the brain processes more quickly is considered conceptually fluent.

While prior exposure can enhance both perceptual and conceptual fluency, the two phenomena are distinct. Perceptual fluency arises when the processing of a stimulus is facilitated by its physical characteristics (Bornstein & D'Agostino, 1994; Jacoby et al., 1989; Janiszewski, 1988, 1990, 1993; Shapiro, 1999), whereas conceptual fluency relates to cases where processing is aided by the stimulus's meaning (Shapiro, 1999; Shapiro et al., 1997; Whittlesea, 1993).

The first experiment to directly examine conceptual fluency's influence on individuals' evaluations was conducted by Whittlesea (1993, Experiment 5). In this study, fluency was manipulated by placing a target word in a semantically predictable or unpredictable context (e.g., "the stormy sea overturned the boat" vs. "the stormy sea threw the lamp"). The final word in the predictable context (boat) was recognized faster than the one in the unpredictable context (lamp). Consequently, when participants rated their preferences for the target words, the semantically predictable word (boat) received a more favorable evaluation than the unpredictable one (lamp), confirming that stimuli with high semantic content elicit more positive evaluations than neutral stimuli. However, Whittlesea's (1993) study did not clarify whether preferences for the target words were influenced by the presence of fluency in the predictive context, its absence in the non-predictive context, or both.

To address these uncertainties, Lee and Labroo (2004) conducted several experiments to explore the role of conceptual fluency in individuals' affective judgments. The first experiment aimed to confirm the effects of fluency on evaluations while ruling out alternative explanations for Whittlesea's findings. This study employed the same procedure, using common words as target stimuli to analyze both perceptual and conceptual fluency. Participants were presented with a sentence, followed by a word that could either match or differ from the target word in the sentence (e.g., "They spent three hours looking at a dress": "dress" or "drink"). As expected, when the target word matched the preceding sentence's last word ("dress"), an increase in perceptual fluency was recorded, leading to a more positive evaluation of the word. Next, the researchers examined the effect of conceptual fluency through two methods: presenting a "predictable" sentence or establishing a semantic association with the last word in the sentence. In the first case, a sentence implied a predictable situation ("The mother immersed the white sweater in water": "water"), making the target word easily accessible and increasing conceptual fluency, which resulted in a more positive affective response. In the second case, a target word semantically related to the last word of the previous sentence ("He wrote numbers on a piece of paper": "pencil") facilitated memory access, leading participants to rate the target word more favorably. Later, participants evaluated the pleasantness of semantically meaningful target words, characterized by a high level of fluency, alongside words that were not preceded by any sentence and thus were neither conceptually nor perceptually fluent.

The results showed that the former elicited a high level of pleasantness, while the latter received a low level, further emphasizing that fluency fosters positive attitudes. In a second experiment, the robustness of fluency effects on evaluations was tested in a marketing context using a familiar consumer product (ketchup) as the target stimulus. Perceptual fluency was manipulated through prior exposure to the product, and conceptual fluency was adjusted by influencing participants' expectations of encountering the product. Participants were exposed to either a condition of high conceptual and perceptual fluency or low conceptual and perceptual fluency. The results supported the idea that both types of fluency contribute to forming more positive attitudes. Specifically, attitudes were more favorable when the product was made more accessible in memory, even without prior exposure, such as when a complementary product (mayonnaise) was shown instead of the target product (ketchup), creating a condition of high conceptual fluency and low perceptual fluency.

In a final study, it was demonstrated that the effects of conceptual fluency are not always positive. When fluency is linked to negative valence, such as recalling undesirable situations, attitudes toward the related stimulus can become unfavorable. To test this hypothesis, an unfamiliar brand with a somewhat negative connotation ("Nutriace Enriching Conditioner") was chosen, with examples like "Not-Nice-to-Lice," a lice-killing shampoo. Participants rated this product unfavorably. Thus, it can be concluded that while prior exposure to a target product fosters a more positive attitude, when conceptual fluency is associated with negative situations, attitudes toward the stimulus or brand may decline.

4 THE ROLE OF AESTHETIC DIMENSIONS AND FLUENCY IN CONSUMER BEHAVIOR

In today's visually driven marketplace, consumers face a constant barrage of choices and must quickly navigate competing options. Aesthetic qualities often serve as heuristics, enabling consumers to evaluate a product's potential satisfaction without engaging in detailed analysis. Numerous studies have investigated how specific design aspects—such as simplicity, balance, and complexity—affect consumer preferences. This body of research indicates that aesthetics not only influence initial attraction but also contribute to different marketing contexts, such as product design, retailing, advertising, branding, and logo design.

For instance, research in product design reveals the significant impact of aesthetic dimensions on consumer behavior. A particular studied dimension is size, in fact, larger products or packaging are often perceived as having greater value and better quality, a phenomenon known as the size-to-value heuristic, where consumers associate size with substance and utility (Raghubir & Krishna, 1999).

Moreover, packaging in brighter or more saturated colors tends to stand out more on shelves, increasing consumer attention and purchase likelihood (Garber et al., 2000). Bloch et al. (2003) developed a framework to assess individual differences in the importance of visual aesthetics in purchasing decisions. Their findings indicate that consumers who prioritize aesthetics are more likely to gravitate toward visually appealing products, associating them with higher functionality and quality.

Similarly, Creusen and Schoormans (2005) explored how product appearance influences consumer choice. Their research found that design elements such as form, color, and material significantly impact judgments about usability and performance. For example, smooth surfaces and rounded shapes are often perceived as user-friendly, while sharp edges or irregular shapes may suggest complexity or sophistication. The concepts of symmetry and balance in design have also been extensively studied. Hekkert (2006) suggested that consumers are naturally drawn to designs exhibiting harmony and balance, as these attributes evoke a sense of order and predictability, often linked to positive emotional responses. This aligns with Gestalt psychology, which posits that people tend to perceive whole forms rather than individual components (see Wertheimer, 1938). Consequently, symmetrical or balanced designs are generally regarded as more aesthetically pleasing, fostering a stronger emotional connection with the product and increasing the likelihood of purchase.

In advertising, visual design plays a pivotal role in capturing consumer attention and conveying key brand messages. Elements such as color, composition, typography, and imagery significantly influence how an advertisement is perceived. Firstly, research has shown that larger stimuli are more effective at capturing consumer attention due to their visual prominence, thereby increasing engagement with advertisements. However, excessively large stimuli can overwhelm consumers, potentially resulting in decreased interest or even avoidance (Pieters & Wedel, 2004). Research suggests that aesthetically pleasing ads can increase attention, emotional engagement, and information retention (Pieters et al., 2010). Ads that are too simple may fail to engage viewers, while overly complex ads can be challenging to process, resulting in lower engagement. The ideal level of complexity in advertising design appears to lie in the middle—moderate complexity captures and maintains attention without overwhelming the viewer. Aesthetic qualities in ads evoke emotional responses that can positively affect brand attitudes. For instance, ads that are visually balanced and harmonious lead to better emotional responses and higher recall (Tuch et al., 2012). Moreover, Veryzer and Hutchinson (1998) found that well-designed ads enhance perceptions of product quality and overall brand equity.

In retail environments aesthetics are critical in shaping the overall shopping experience. Elements such as store layout, lighting, color schemes, and product displays influence not only how consumers navigate the store but also their perceptions of the brand and their emotional states.

The concept of atmospherics, introduced by Kotler (1973), highlights how the design and aesthetics of a retail space can influence consumer behavior. A well-designed, aesthetically pleasing store environment leads to longer shopping times, more favorable evaluations, and higher spending (Spence et al., 2014). Visual stimuli such as lighting and color can enhance mood, with warmer colors and softer lighting creating a welcoming atmosphere that increases consumer comfort (Bellizzi & Hite, 1992). Additionally, Chebat and Morrin (2007) explored how the color and texture of mall décor influence consumer perceptions, demonstrating that these environmental cues affect the overall shopping experience. For instance, warm colors tend to evoke comfort, while cooler tones may create a more professional or clinical atmosphere.

Moreover, the aesthetic quality of a retail environment directly impacts consumer perceptions of product quality and the overall store image. Baker et al. (1994) found that aesthetically appealing retail environments make products seem more desirable, thereby enhancing the overall shopping experience.

Branding and logo design offer valuable opportunities to explore how aesthetic dimensions influence consumer behavior. For example, specific colors are often associated with particular emotions or meanings. Blue, for instance, evokes trust and calmness, influencing consumer attitudes toward a brand (Labrecque & Milne, 2012). Elliot and Maier's (2014) comprehensive review expands on this, explaining that the effects of color are shaped by evolutionary, cultural, and contextual factors. For instance, red can evoke feelings of urgency or danger, triggering either approach or avoidance behaviors, while blue often promotes calmness and trust, which can enhance performance or foster positive brand perceptions.

Additionally, research shows that design affects both brand attitudes and long-term loyalty (e.g., Bloch et al., 2003; Veryzer & Hutchinson, 1998). Logos, as central elements of brand identity, often represent the first interaction consumers have with a brand. This makes their visual characteristics critical for establishing recognition and forming lasting associations (Ariely, 2014; Van Grinsven & Das, 2016). Various studies have examined how factors such as simplicity, complexity, and balance affect consumer responses to logos, providing insights into the trade-offs involved in logo design. Henderson and Cote (1998) developed a framework for selecting and modifying logos, emphasizing the need to balance simplicity and uniqueness. Their research suggests that logos with moderate complexity—distinctive yet not overly intricate—are most effective in creating strong brand recognition. Simple logos tend to be processed more quickly and remembered more easily, which is essential for brands aiming for quick recall. However, overly simplistic logos may lack the distinctiveness necessary to differentiate a brand in a crowded market.

Miceli et al. (2014) studied how visual and conceptual complexity in logo design influences consumer evaluations across multiple exposures. Their findings revealed that while complex logos might initially be more difficult to process, repeated exposure can enhance consumer engagement and attachment to the brand. This suggests that while simplicity aids initial recognition, complexity can foster deeper cognitive processing and long-term brand loyalty, particularly in industries with frequent consumer interactions, such as fashion or technology.

In line with this, Van Grinsven and Das (2016) found that logo complexity moderates the effects of exposure on brand recognition and attitudes. Logos with moderate complexity were more effective at generating positive brand attitudes after repeated exposure. While simpler logos are often favored for their ease of recognition, moderate complexity can foster a stronger emotional connection with consumers over time.

Bossel et al. (2019) examined trends in brand logo design and found that while simple logos are increasingly favored for their modern, minimalistic appeal, they may reduce the perceived premium nature of certain brands. This suggests that while simplicity is often effective, particularly in digital media, it may not align with a brand's positioning strategy—especially for luxury or high-end brands, where complexity can signal exclusivity and craftsmanship.

Beyond basic design elements, fluency has emerged as a critical factor in understanding consumer responses to visual stimuli. Simpler, more familiar designs are typically processed more fluently than complex or unfamiliar ones (Reber et al., 2004). When a product's design is easily processed, it creates a sense of comfort and familiarity, often biasing consumers toward that product.

Reber et al. (2004) conducted studies investigating how processing fluency influences aesthetic pleasure. Their findings showed that individuals tend to prefer visual stimuli that are processed with greater ease, as these stimuli evoke positive emotional responses. In one experiment, participants rated abstract paintings, consistently favoring those with simpler compositions or familiar patterns over more complex ones. This underscores the importance of simplicity in design, especially when immediate consumer appeal is the goal.

Mauri et al. (2021) examined the impact of front-of-package (FOP) nutrition labels on consumer preferences for low-sugar products, finding that simpler, more fluent label designs helped consumers quickly identify healthier options. This demonstrates that fluency in label design reduces cognitive effort in processing nutritional information, leading to more accurate decision-making.

Similarly, Novemsky et al. (2007) explored how fluency influences consumer choice across various product categories. They found that consumers tend to prefer products that are easier to process, even if they are not necessarily superior in quality. This preference for fluent options was particularly strong in scenarios with many choices, where cognitive load increased the appeal of easily processed products. This underscores the importance of fluency in product design and packaging—especially in contexts requiring quick decision-making. Chan and Northey (2021) found that luxury products presented in visually fluent settings were more likely to be favored by consumers. However, they noted that while fluency facilitates ease of processing, a degree of complexity is necessary to maintain the sense of exclusivity expected in luxury branding. This delicate balance ensures that luxury brands remain cognitively accessible while conveying their premium status.

The importance of visual design has been demonstrated to play a pivotal role also in eco-label logos evaluations. Research by Donato and

Adıgüzel (2022) highlights the impact of visual complexity in eco-labels, suggesting that while simplicity is often associated with clarity and ease of understanding, it is not always the optimal choice. Their study demonstrates that a balanced approach to visual complexity can enhance product evaluations in online settings, challenging the notion that simpler designs are universally better.

The design of eco-labels must strike a delicate balance between simplicity and informative content. Tang et al. (2004) emphasize the importance of integrating both visual and verbal elements to effectively communicate the environmental benefits of a product. They argue that an eco-label should not only be visually appealing but also include concise messaging that resonates with eco-conscious consumers. This integration allows consumers to quickly comprehend the value of the eco-label, fostering a sense of trust and credibility. Furthermore, Rihn et al. (2019) explored how the format of eco-labels—whether textual or graphical—affects consumers' visual attention and willingness to pay. Their findings indicate that logo-based eco-labels capture greater visual attention compared to text-only labels, which enhances consumers' willingness to pay a premium for products associated with strong visual branding. This highlights the need for brands to prioritize logo design in their sustainability messaging, ensuring that eco-labels stand out in a crowded marketplace. Visual design also plays a pivotal role in establishing brand identity and fostering emotional connections with consumers. According to Van Loo et al. (2015), sustainability labels on products such as coffee have been shown to influence consumer preferences and willingness to pay. The aesthetic appeal of these labels, combined with a clear representation of sustainability attributes, can evoke positive feelings toward the brand and its products. Eco-labels that effectively utilize color, shape, and imagery can create an immediate emotional response, facilitating a deeper engagement with the brand's sustainability narrative.

In the context of green advertising, Donato and Adıgüzel (2024) provide practical guidelines for creating effective eco-labels that resonate with consumers. They analyzed how visual and conceptual complexity, alongside factors such as color and the amount of text, influences the evaluation of eco-labels, particularly through the lens of processing fluency. By understanding these dynamics, eco-label designers can enhance their designs to create more impactful labels.

In conclusion, while the current body of research underscores the critical role of visual design in shaping consumer perceptions, there remains a pressing need for further investigation, particularly in the sustainability domain. Understanding how aesthetic qualities influence consumers' evaluations of eco-labels and their subsequent purchase intentions is vital for effectively communicating a brand's commitment to environmental responsibility. The findings of previous studies suggest that an optimal balance between simplicity and complexity, alongside engaging storytelling elements, can enhance the impact of eco-labels in a competitive marketplace. The next chapter will delve into an empirical study focused on eco-label logo design, providing insights into how various design elements affect sustainability perceptions and consumer behavior. This exploration aims to contribute to the growing body of knowledge on the intersection of visual design and sustainability, ultimately guiding brands in their efforts to create meaningful connections with eco-conscious consumers.

REFERENCES

Airey, D. (2014). *Logo design love: A guide to creating iconic brand identities.* Peachpit Press.

Alter, A. L., & Oppenheimer, D. M. (2009). Uniting the tribes of fluency to form a metacognitive nation. *Personality and Social Psychology Review, 13*(3), 219–235.

Amatulli, C., De Angelis, M., & Donato, C. (2020). An investigation on the effectiveness of hedonic versus utilitarian message appeals in luxury product communication. *Psychology & Marketing, 37*(4), 523–534.

Anderson, P. W. (1972). More is different: Broken symmetry and the nature of the hierarchical structure of science. *Science, 177*(4047), 393–396.

Arnheim, R. (1943). Gestalt and art. *The Journal of Aesthetics and Art Criticism, 2*(8), 71–75.

Baker, G., & Franken, R. (1967). Effects of stimulus size, brightness and complexity upon EEG desynchronization. *Psychonomic Science, 7*(9), 289–290.

Baker, J., Grewal, D., & Parasuraman, A. (1994). The influence of store environment on quality inferences and store image. *Journal of the Academy of Marketing Science, 22*, 328–339.

Ball, V. K. (1965). The aesthetics of color: A review of fifty years of experimentation. *The Journal of Aesthetics and Art Criticism, 23*(4), 441–452.

Bellizzi, J. A., & Hite, R. E. (1992). Environmental color, consumer feelings, and purchase likelihood. *Psychology & Marketing, 9*(5), 347–363.

Berger, J., & Milkman, K. L. (2012). What makes online content viral? *Journal of Marketing Research, 49*(2), 192–205.

Berlyne, D. E. (1971). *Aesthetics and psychobiology.* Appleton-Century-Croft of Merdith Corporation.

Berlyne, D. E. (1958). The influence of complexity and novelty in visual figures on orienting responses. *Journal of Experimental Psychology, 55*(3), 289.

Berlyne, D. E. (1960). Novelty, uncertainty, conflict, complexity. In D. E. Berlyne, *Conflict, arousal, and curiosity* (pp. 18–44). McGraw-Hill Book Company.

Berlyne, D. E. (1970). Novelty, complexity, and hedonic value. *Perception & Psychophysics, 8*(5), 279–286.

Berlyne, D. E., & Borsa, D. M. (1968). Uncertainty and the orientation reaction. *Perception & Psychophysics, 3*(1), 77–79.

Berlyne, D. E., & Boudewijns, W. J. (1971). Hedonic effects of uniformity in variety. *Canadian Journal of Psychology/revue Canadienne De Psychologie, 25*(3), 195.

Berlyne, D. E., & Crozier, J. B. (1971). Effects of complexity and prechoice stimulation on exploratory choice. *Perception & Psychophysics, 10*(4), 242–246.

Berlyne, D. E., & Lewis, J. L. (1963). Effects of heightened arousal on human exploratory behaviour. *Canadian Journal of Psychology/revue Canadienne De Psychologie, 17*(4), 398.

Berlyne, D. E., & McDonnell, P. (1965). Effects of stimulus complexity and incongruity on duration of EEG desynchronization. *Electroencephalography & Clinical Neurophysiology.*

Berlyne, D. E., & Parham, L. C. C. (1968). Determinants of subjective novelty. *Perception & Psychophysics, 3*, 415–423.

Berlyne, D. E., Craw, M. A., Salapatek, P. H., & Lewis, J. L. (1963). Novelty, complexity, incongruity, extrinsic motivation, and the GSR. *Journal of Experimental Psychology, 66*(6), 560.

Berlyne, D. E., Ogilvie, J. C., & Parham, L. C. (1968). The dimensionality of visual complexity, interestingness, and pleasingness. *Canadian Journal of Psychology/revue Canadienne De Psychologie, 22*(5), 376.

Berlyne, D. E. (1961). Conflict and the orientation reaction. *Journal of Experimental Psychology,* 157–169.

Berlyne, D. E. (1966). Les Mesures de la Preference Estétique, Sciences de l'Art, N.3, PP. 9–22.

Bloch, P. H., Brunel, F. F., & Arnold, T. J. (2003). Individual differences in the centrality of visual product aesthetics: Concept and measurement. *Journal of Consumer Research, 29*(4), 551–565.

Bornstein, R. F., & D'agostino, P. R. (1992). Stimulus recognition and the mere exposure effect. *Journal of Personality and Social Psychology, 63*(4), 545.

Bornstein, R. F., & D'Agostino, P. R. (1994). The attribution and discounting of perceptual fluency: Preliminary tests of a perceptual fluency/attributional model of the mere exposure effect. *Social Cognition, 12*(2), 103–128.

Bossel, V., Geyskens, K., & Goukens, C. (2019). Facing a trend of brand logo simplicity: The impact of brand logo design on consumption. *Food Quality and Preference, 71*, 129–135.

Bryson, J. B., & Driver, M. J. (1972). Cognitive complexity, introversion, and preference for complexity. *Journal of Personality and Social Psychology, 23*(3), 320.

Cacioppo, J. T., Petty, R. E., Losch, M. E., & Kim, H. S. (1986). Electromyographic activity over facial muscle regions can differentiate the valence and intensity of affective reactions. *Journal of Personality and Social Psychology, 50*(2), 260.

Chan, E. Y., & Northey, G. (2021). Luxury goods in online retail: How high/low positioning influences consumer processing fluency and preference. *Journal of Business Research, 132*, 136–145.

Chebat, J. C., & Morrin, M. (2007). Colors and cultures: Exploring the effects of mall décor on consumer perceptions. *Journal of Business Research, 60*(3), 189–196.

Checkosky, S. F., & Whitlock, D. (1973). Effects of pattern goodness on recognition time in a memory search task. *Journal of Experimental Psychology, 100*(2), 341.

Creusen, M. E., & Schoormans, J. P. (2005). The different roles of product appearance in consumer choice. *Journal of Product Innovation Management, 22*(1), 63–81.

Day, H. (1968). The importance of symmetry and complexity in the evaluation of complexity, interest and pleasingness. *Psychonomic Science, 10*(10), 339–340.

Day, H. Y. (1966). Looking time as a function of stimulus variables and individual differences. *Perceptual and Motor Skills, 22*(2), 423–428.

Day, H. Y. (1967). Evaluations of subjective complexity, pleasingness and interestingness for a series of random polygons varying in complexity. *Perception & Psychophysics, 2*, 281–286.

Desimone, R., Miller, E. K., Chelazzi, L., & Lueschow, A. (1995). Multiple memory systems in the visual cortex.

Donato, C., & Adıgüzel, F. (2022). Visual complexity of eco-labels and product evaluations in online setting: Is simple always better? *Journal of Retailing and Consumer Services, 67*, 102961.

Donato, C., & Adıgüzel, F. (2024). The effects of visual design on eco-labels evaluations: Guidelines for effective green advertising. *Journal of Marketing Theory and Practice*, 1–18.

Eisenman, R. (1969). Creativity and academic major: Business versus English majors. *Journal of Applied Psychology, 53*(5), 392.

Elliot, A. J., & Maier, M. A. (2014). Color psychology: Effects of perceiving color on psychological functioning in humans. *Annual Review of Psychology, 65*, 95–120.

Eysenck, H. J. (1941). The empirical determination of an aesthetic formula. *Psychological Review, 48*(1), 83.

Eysenck, H. J., & Tunstall, O. (1968). La personalité et l'esthétique des formes simples [Personality and the aesthetics of simple forms]. *Sciences De'art, 5,* 3–9.

Fairchild, M. D. (2013). *Color appearance models.* John Wiley & Sons.

Feagin, S. F. (1995). Beauty. In R. Audi (Ed.), *The Cambridge dictionary of philosophy* (p. 66). Cambridge University Press.

Freeman, D. (2010). Aesthetic experience as the transformation of pleasure. *The Harvard Review of Philosophy, 17*(1), 56–75.

Garber, L. L., Burke, R. R., & Jones, J. M. (2000). *The role of package color in consumer purchase consideration and choice* (pp. 1–46). Marketing Science Institute.

Garner, W. R. (2014). *The processing of information and structure.* Psychology Press.

Gibson, D., Baker, G., & Rathie, E. (1967). Effects of size-brightness and complexity of non-meaningful stimulus material on EEG desynchronization. *Psychonomic Science, 8*(11), 503–504.

Gombrich, E. H. (2023). Art and Illusion: A study in the psychology of pictorial representation-Millennium Edition.

Groves, P. M., & Thompson, R. F. (1970). Habituation: A dual-process theory. *Psychological Review, 77*(5), 419.

Guilford, J. P. (1934). The affective value of color as a function of hue, tint, and chroma. *Journal of Experimental Psychology, 17*(3), 342.

Guilford, J. P. (1940). An inventory of factors STDC R.

Haber, R. N., & Hershenson, M. (1965). Effects of repeated brief exposures on the growth of a percept. *Journal of Experimental Psychology, 69*(1), 40.

Haywood, H. C., & Hunt, J. (1963). Effects of epinephrine upon novelty preference and arousal. *The Journal of Abnormal and Social Psychology, 67*(3), 206.

Hekkert, P. (2006). Design aesthetics: Principles of pleasure in design. *Psychology Science, 48*(2), 157.

Hekkert, P., & van Wieringen, P. C. (1996). The impact of level of expertise on the evaluation of original and altered versions of post-impressionistic paintings. *Acta psychologica, 94*(2), 117–131.

Helson, H., & Lansford, T. (1970). The role of spectral energy of source and background color in the pleasantness of object colors. *Applied Optics, 9*(7), 1513–1562.

Henderson, P. W., & Cote, J. A. (1998). Guidelines for selecting or modifying logos. *Journal of Marketing, 62*(2), 14–30.

Hoats, D. L., Miller, M. B., & Spitz, H. H. (1963). Experiments on perceptual curiosity in mental retardates and normals. *American Journal of Mental Deficiency*.

Houston, J. P., Garskof, B. E., & Silber, D. E. (1965). The informational basis of judged complexity. *The Journal of General Psychology, 72*(2), 277–284.

Humphrey, D. (1997). Preferences in symmetries and symmetries in drawings: Asymmetries between ages and sexes. *Empirical Studies of the Arts, 15*(1), 41–60.

Huntley, H. E. (2012). *The divine proportion*. Courier Corporation.

Ingarden, R., & McCormick, P. J. (1985). Selected papers in aesthetics. *Journal of Aesthetics and Art Criticism, 45*(1).

Jacoby, L. L. (1983). Remembering the data: Analyzing interactive processes in reading. *Journal of Verbal Learning and Verbal Behavior, 22*(5), 485–508.

Jacoby, L. L., & Dallas, M. (1981). On the relationship between autobiographical memory and perceptual learning. *Journal of Experimental Psychology: General, 110*(3), 306.

Janiszewski, C. (1988). Preconscious processing effects: The independence of attitude formation and conscious thought. *Journal of Consumer Research, 15*(2), 199–209.

Janiszewski, C. (1990). The influence of print advertisement organization on affect toward a brand name. *Journal of Consumer Research, 17*(1), 53–65.

Janiszewski, C. (1993). Preattentive mere exposure effects. *Journal of Consumer Research, 20*(3), 376–392.

Janiszewski, C., & Meyvis, T. (2001). Effects of brand logo complexity, repetition, and spacing on processing fluency and judgment. *Journal of Consumer Research, 28*(1), 18–32.

Jones, A., Wilkinson, H. J., & Braden, I. (1961). Information deprivation as a motivational variable. *Journal of Experimental Psychology, 62*(2), 126.

Jost, J. T., Kruglanski, A. W., & Nelson, T. O. (2013). Social metacognition: An expansionist review. In *Metacognition* (pp. 137–154). Psychology Press.

Karmel, B. Z. (1969). The effect of age, complexity, and amount of contour on pattern preferences in human infants. *Journal of Experimental Child Psychology, 7*(2), 339–354.

Kelley, C. M., & Jacoby, L. L. (1990). The construction of subjective experience: Memory attributions. *Mind & Language, 5*(1), 49–68.

Kelley, C. M., & Jacoby, L. L. (1998). Subjective reports and process dissociation: Fluency, knowing, and feeling. *Acta Psychologica, 98*(2–3), 127–140.

Klinger, M. R., & Greenwald, A. G. (1994). Preferences need no inferences?: The cognitive basis of unconscious mere exposure effects.

Koffka, K. (2013). *Principles of gestalt psychology*. Routledge.

Kotler, P. (1973). Atmospherics as a marketing tool. *Journal of Retailing, 49*(4), 48–64.

Labrecque, L. I., & Milne, G. R. (2012). Exciting red and competent blue: The importance of color in marketing. *Journal of the Academy of Marketing Science, 40*(5), 711–727.

Lalo, C. (1908). *L'esthétique expérimentale contemporaine.* F. Alcan.

Lang, P. J., Greenwald, M. K., Bradley, M. M., & Hamm, A. O. (1993). Looking at pictures: Affective, facial, visceral, and behavioral reactions. *Psychophysiology, 30*(3), 261–273.

Leckart, B. T. (1966). Looking time: The effects of stimulus complexity and familiarity. *Perception & Psychophysics, 1,* 142–144.

Leckart, B. T., Gehres, L., & Thornton, G. (1970). Looking time: Experimenter and instruction effects. *Perception & Psychophysics, 8,* 54–56.

Lee, A. Y., & Labroo, A. A. (2004). The effect of conceptual and perceptual fluency on brand evaluation. *Journal of Marketing Research, 41*(2), 151–165.

Lewenstein, M., & Nowak, A. (1989). Recognition with self-control in neural networks. *Physical Review A, 40*(8), 4652.

Lidwell, W., Holden, K., & Butler, J. (2010). *Universal principles of design, revised and updated: 125 ways to enhance usability, influence perception, increase appeal, make better design decisions, and teach through design.* Rockport Pub.

Mackworth, N. H., & Bruner, J. S. (1966). *Selecting visual information during recognition by adults and children.* Harvard center for cognitive studies.

Mackworth, N. H., & Morandi, A. J. (1967). The gaze selects informative details within pictures. *Perception & Psychophysics, 2*(11), 547–552.

Mandler, G., Nakamura, Y., & Van Zandt, B. J. (1987). Nonspecific effects of exposure on stimuli that cannot be recognized. *Journal of Experimental Psychology: Learning, Memory, and Cognition, 13*(4), 646.

Marin, M. M. (2022). The role of collative variables in aesthetic experiences. *The Oxford Handbook of Empirical Aesthetics,* 385.

Martin, L. J. (1906). An experimental study of Fechner's principles of aesthetics. *Psychological Review, 13*(3), 142.

Martindale, C., & Moore, K. (1989). Relationship of musical preference to collative, ecological, and psychophysical variables. *Music Perception, 6*(4), 431–445.

Mauri, C., Grazzini, L., Ulqinaku, A., & Poletti, E. (2021). The effect of front-of-package nutrition labels on the choice of low sugar products. *Psychology & Marketing, 38*(8), 1323–1339.

Mazzoni, G., & Nelson, T. O. (1995). Judgments of learning are affected by the kind of encoding in ways that cannot be attributed to the level of recall. *Journal of Experimental Psychology: Learning, Memory, and Cognition, 21*(5), 1263.

McGlone, M. S., & Tofighbakhsh, J. (2000). Birds of a feather flock conjointly (?): Rhyme as reason in aphorisms. *Psychological Science, 11*(5), 424–428.

Metcalfe, J., & Shimamura, A. P. (Eds.). (1994). *Metacognition: Knowing about knowing*. MIT press.

Miceli, G. N., Scopelliti, I., Raimondo, M. A., & Donato, C. (2014). Breaking through complexity: Visual and conceptual dimensions in logo evaluation across exposures. *Psychology & Marketing, 31*(10), 886–899.

Mindus, L. A. (1968). *The role of redundancy and complexity in the perception of tonal patterns* (Doctoral dissertation). Clark University.

Mirbach, D. (2009). Magnitudo aesthetica, aesthetic greatness. Ethical aspects of Alexander Gottlieb Baumgarten's Fragmentary Aesthetica. *The Nordic Journal of Aesthetics, 20*(36–37).

Morreall, J. (1983). *Taking laughter seriously*. State University of New York.

Munsinger, H., & Kessen, W. (1964). Uncertainty, structure, and preference. *Psychological Monographs: General and Applied, 78*(9), 1.

Murray, M. (1989). Ingarden and the end of phenomenological aesthetics. *Research in phenomenology*, 171–179.

Norman, K. A., O'Reilly, R. C., & Huber, D. E. (2000, January). Modeling neocortical contributions to recognition memory. In *The cognitive neuroscience meeting*.

Novemsky, N., Dhar, R., Schwarz, N., & Simonson, I. (2007). Preference fluency in choice. *Journal of Marketing Research, 44*(3), 347–356.

Nunnally, J. C., Faw, T. T., & Bashford, M. B. (1969). Effect of degrees of incongruity on visual fixations in children and adults. *Journal of Experimental Psychology, 81*(2), 360.

Palmer, S. E. (1991). Goodness, gestalt, groups, and garner: Local symmetry subgroups as a theory of figural goodness.

Palmer, S. E., & Schloss, K. B. (2010). An ecological valence theory of human color preference. *Proceedings of the National Academy of Sciences, 107*(19), 8877–8882.

Pierce, E. (1895). *The aesthetics of simple forms* (Doctoral dissertation). Harvard University.

Pieters, R., & Wedel, M. (2004). Attention capture and transfer in advertising: Brand, pictorial, and text-size effects. *Journal of Marketing, 68*(2), 36–50.

Pieters, R., Wedel, M., & Batra, R. (2010). The stopping power of advertising: Measures and effects of visual complexity. *Journal of Marketing, 74*(5), 48–60.

Posner, M. I., & Keele, S. W. (1968). On the genesis of abstract ideas. *Journal of Experimental Psychology, 77*(3p1), 353.

Puffer, E. D. (1903). Studies in symmetry. *The psychological review: Monograph supplements*.

Raghubir, P., & Krishna, A. (1999). Vital dimensions in volume perception: Can the eye fool the stomach? *Journal of Marketing Research, 36*(3), 313–326.

Reber, R., Schwarz, N., & Winkielman, P. (2004). Processing fluency and aesthetic pleasure: Is beauty in the perceiver's processing experience? *Personality and Social Psychology Review, 8*(4), 364–382.

Reber, R., Winkielman, P., & Schwarz, N. (1998). Effects of perceptual fluency on affective judgments. *Psychological Science, 9*(1), 45–48.

Rihn, A., Wei, X., & Khachatryan, H. (2019). Text vs. logo: Does eco-label format influence consumers' visual attention and willingness-to-pay for fruit plants? An experimental auction approach. *Journal of Behavioral and Experimental Economics, 82*, 101452.

Roediger, H. L. (1990). Implicit memory: Retention without remembering. *American Psychologist, 45*(9), 1043.

Schwarz, N. (2013). Accessible content and accessibility experiences: The interplay of declarative and experiential information in judgment. In *Metacognition* (pp. 87–99). Psychology Press.

Seamon, J. G., Brody, N., & Kauff, D. M. (1983). Affective discrimination of stimuli that are not recognized: Effects of shadowing, masking, and cerebral laterality. *Journal of Experimental Psychology: Learning, Memory, and Cognition, 9*(3), 544.

Shapiro, S. (1999). When an ad's influence is beyond our conscious control: Perceptual and conceptual fluency effects caused by incidental ad exposure. *Journal of Consumer Research, 26*(1), 16–36.

Shapiro, S., MacInnis, D. J., & Heckler, S. E. (1997). The effects of incidental ad exposure on the formation of consideration sets. *Journal of Consumer Research, 24*(1), 94–104.

Silvera, D. H., Josephs, R. A., & Giesler, R. B. (2002). Bigger is better: The influence of physical size on aesthetic preference judgments. *Journal of Behavioral Decision Making, 15*(3), 189–202.

Silvia, P. J. (2012). Human emotions and aesthetic experience. *Aesthetic science: connecting minds, brain and experience* (pp. 250–275).

Solso, R. L. (1994). *Cognition and the visual arts.* MIT press.

Spence, C., Puccinelli, N. M., Grewal, D., & Roggeveen, A. L. (2014). Store atmospherics: A multisensory perspective. *Psychology & Marketing, 31*(7), 472–488.

Tang, E., Fryxell, G. E., & Chow, C. S. (2004). Visual and verbal communication in the design of eco-label for green consumer products. *Journal of International Consumer Marketing, 16*(4), 85–105.

Tatarkiewicz, W. (1970). Did aesthetics progress? *Philosophy and Phenomenological Research, 31*(1), 47–59.

Thorndike, E. L. (1917). Individual differences in judgments of the beauty of simple forms. *Psychological Review, 24*(2), 147.

Tuch, A. N., Presslaber, E. E., Stöcklin, M., Opwis, K., & Bargas-Avila, J. A. (2012). The role of visual complexity and prototypicality regarding first impression of websites: Working towards understanding aesthetic judgments. *International Journal of Human-Computer Studies, 70*(11), 794–811.

Tulving, E., & Schacter, D. L. (1990). Priming and human memory systems. *Science, 247*(4940), 301–306.

Tversky, A., & Kahneman, D. (1973). Availability: A heuristic for judging frequency and probability. *Cognitive Psychology, 5*(2), 207–232.

Van Grinsven, B., & Das, E. (2016). Logo design in marketing communications: Brand logo complexity moderates exposure effects on brand recognition and brand attitude. *Journal of Marketing Communications, 22*(3), 256–270.

Van Loo, E. J., Caputo, V., Nayga, R. M., Jr., Seo, H. S., Zhang, B., & Verbeke, W. (2015). Sustainability labels on coffee: Consumer preferences, willingness-to-pay and visual attention to attributes. *Ecological Economics, 118*, 215–225.

Veryzer, R. W., Jr., & Hutchinson, J. W. (1998). The influence of unity and prototypicality on aesthetic responses to new product designs. *Journal of Consumer Research, 24*(4), 374–394.

Wertheimer, M. (1938). Gestalt psychology. *Source book of gestalt psychology.* Harcourt, Brace and Co.

Whittlesea, B. W. (1993). Illusions of familiarity. *Journal of Experimental Psychology: Learning, Memory, and Cognition, 19*(6), 1235.

Whittlesea, B. W., Jacoby, L. L., & Girard, K. (1990). Illusions of immediate memory: Evidence of an attributional basis for feelings of familiarity and perceptual quality. *Journal of Memory and Language, 29*(6), 716–732.

Wilson, S. D. (1966). A reflection-diffraction microscope for observing diatoms in color. *Applied Optics, 5*(10), 1683–1684.

Winkielman, P., & Cacioppo, J. T. (2001). Mind at ease puts a smile on the face: Psychophysiological evidence that processing facilitation elicits positive affect. *Journal of Personality and Social Psychology, 81*(6), 989.

Witherspoon, D., & Allan, L. G. (1985). The effect of a prior presentation on temporal judgments in a perceptual identification task. *Memory & Cognition, 13*(2), 101–111.

Witmer, L. (1894). *Psychological literature: Æsthetics of form.*

Yarbus, A. L. (2013). *Eye movements and vision.* Springer.

Zajonc, R. B. (1968). Attitudinal effects of mere exposure. *Journal of Personality and Social Psychology, 9*(2p2), 1.

Zeising, A. (1855). Äesthetische Forschungen [Aesthetic Research]. *Frankfort: Medinger.*

CHAPTER 4

The Effect of Eco-Label Logos Visual Design on Consumers' Sustainability Perceptions: An Empirical Study

Abstract This chapter examines the role of eco-label design in shaping consumers' perceptions of sustainability and their adoption of labels. It begins with a review of literature on sustainability perceptions, aesthetic dimensions in visual communication, and eco-label design. The chapter then presents an empirical study involving 15 real Type I eco-labels, analyzing how visual dimensions—such as visual complexity, conceptual complexity, background color, and text amount—affect consumers' sustainability perceptions and label adoption. The results reveal that consumers perceive visually complex yet conceptually simple eco-labels with green or blue backgrounds and explanatory text as more sustainable and are more likely to adopt them.

Keywords Eco-label design · Visual complexity · Conceptual complexity · Color background · Text amount · Sustainability perceptions

1   Introduction

Eco-labels have become an essential tool for communicating the sustainability credentials of products to consumers (e.g., Atkinson & Rosenthal, 2014; Thøgersen et al., 2010). As sustainability becomes a key driver of purchasing decisions (Deloitte, 2023[1]), companies and organizations rely on eco-labels to signal their commitment to environmentally and socially responsible practices (e.g., Atkinson & Rosenthal, 2014; Donato & Adigüzel, 2022). However, despite their pivotal role in signaling sustainable purchases, as already noted in the last paragraph of Chapter 2, a significant body of research has shown that consumers often lack awareness or a clear understanding of what eco-labels represent (e.g., Donato & D'Aniello, 2022; Eldesouky et al., 2020; Grunert et al., 2014; Meyerding & Merz, 2018; Song et al., 2019; Xin & Long, 2023). This lack of understanding can result in confusion over their credibility and relevance, ultimately weakening their intended impact (e.g., Ní Choisdealbha et al., 2020).

To be noticed and understood by consumers in everyday purchasing decisions—often involving quick judgments based on visual cues (e.g., Dijksterhuis et al., 2005)—eco-labels must be designed to ensure both recognition and comprehension of their sustainability message. Given the importance of aesthetic dimensions in consumers' evaluations (see Chapter 3), it is essential to investigate how the visual elements that constitute eco-label logos influence consumers' perceptions of these labels.

Consequently, this chapter delves into the largely unexplored territory of how the visual design of eco-label logos influences consumer perceptions. As already noted, prior research has partially addressed the role of visual elements in shaping consumer attitudes toward eco-labels. For instance, Tang et al. (2004) found that both visual and verbal elements of eco-labels affect the purchase of sustainable products. Donato and Adigüzel (2022) further demonstrated that while design complexity enhances product evaluations by increasing perceptual fluency, feature complexity improves evaluations through conceptual fluency. In a more recent study, Donato and Adigüzel (2024) found that visual complexity,

---

[1] https://www.deloitte.com/uk/en/Industries/consumer/research/sustainable-consumer.html.

green color, and the amount of text positively affect attitudes toward eco-labels, whereas conceptual complexity has a negative impact.

Despite these findings, no research, to the best of the author's knowledge, has focused on investigating how specific design features of eco-label logos effectively communicate their underlying meaning: sustainability. Therefore, particularly relevant for eco-label logos and their sustainable messaging: visual complexity—defined as the variety of visual information present in a stimulus (Berlyne, 1970)—conceptual complexity—referring to a visual stimulus's ability to evoke multiple meanings without a universally accepted one (Perussia, 1988)—as well as color and textual information.

To address the aforementioned gap in the literature, this chapter will first review the literature on visual design and sustainability perceptions, providing a foundation for understanding how aesthetic elements in design influence consumer attitudes toward sustainability. Following this, the chapter will examine the role of logos in shaping consumer perceptions, particularly in terms of sustainability and brand identity. Based on the insights from these literature reviews, hypotheses will be developed to guide the empirical investigation.

Then the chapter will present an empirical study examining how the design (i.e., color, textual information, and visual and conceptual complexity) of eco-label logos influences consumers' sustainability perceptions and label adoption. The applied methodology begins with the design and execution of two pre-tests, followed by a large-scale survey. Real eco-label logos were used to ensure the findings' practical relevance. In the pre-tests, eco-label logos were assessed for their visual complexity and conceptual complexity. This helped identify the appropriate stimuli measurements for the main study, where consumers were asked to evaluate the sustainability and adoption associated with real-life eco-labels. The chapter proceeds to present the findings, which shed light on how different visual characteristics of eco-label logos influence consumers' sustainability perceptions and the discussion of these findings.

2   Theoretical Background

2.1   Sustainability Perceptions and Aesthetic Dimensions in Visual Communication

In the expanding field of sustainable design, the relationship between aesthetics and sustainability perceptions has gained increasing attention. As global awareness of environmental issues grows, visual cues in packaging, branding, and design have become pivotal in shaping consumer attitudes and behaviors toward sustainability (Donato et al., 2021; Magnier et al, 2016). Gallopín et al. (2014) offer a conceptual framework for understanding sustainability through visual interpretations, emphasizing that sustainability can be conveyed through various visual elements, including icons, symbols, and color schemes that evoke a sense of harmony with nature. For instance, green and blue hues are often linked to environmental friendliness, while symbols such as leaves, trees, or water droplets commonly represent sustainability. However, these cues are not universally understood, and their effectiveness is shaped by the cultural background and personal values of consumers.

Ji and Lin (2022) introduce the concept of "emotionally durable design" as a strategy to enhance perceptions of sustainability through aesthetics. They argue that sustainable design should not only address the functional aspects of a product's environmental impact but also its aesthetic appeal, fostering a sense of attachment and responsibility toward the product. In this approach, aesthetics serve as a tool to promote sustainability, influencing consumer behavior and encouraging long-term product use, rather than simply focusing on resource efficiency.

Nickel and Böhm (2024) highlight that minimalist designs are often perceived as more sustainable, as they are associated with waste reduction and essential functionality. This aligns with sustainable consumption principles, which advocate for reduced material use and durability over excess. Majer et al. (2022) similarly point out that visual transparency, both in design and labeling, is key to building consumer trust in sustainability claims. Therefore, products with overly complex or visually cluttered designs can lead to confusion and skepticism, prompting consumers to question the authenticity of sustainability credentials.

Wang et al. (2024) explore the impact of packaging design on consumers' perceptions of eco-friendliness, focusing on visual complexity. Their study shows that simpler packaging designs—characterized by minimal text, clean lines, and fewer graphic elements—are more likely to be seen as environmentally friendly. This perception stems from the ease of processing simpler designs (high fluency), which creates positive associations with sustainability. On the other hand, visually complex packaging, with elaborate graphics or bright colors, is often linked to wastefulness and inefficiency, undermining perceptions of eco-friendliness. The authors note that this effect is especially pronounced among consumers with higher environmental awareness, making simplicity an effective visual strategy for brands targeting eco-conscious audiences.

Beyond product packaging, visual design also plays a critical role in shaping perceptions of sustainability labels. Majer et al. (2022) conducted a systematic review of empirical literature on visual sustainability labels, examining how eco-labels or green certifications influence consumer perceptions and behavior. Their findings show that labels clearly communicating sustainability claims can significantly impact purchasing decisions. However, the effectiveness of these labels depends heavily on their visual clarity, credibility, and consumers' familiarity with their meaning.

2.2 Eco-Labels Visual Design and Hypotheses Development

Aesthetic has been particularly studied in terms of brand logos effectiveness (e.g., Henderson & Cote, 1998; Miceli et al., 2014). For example, Henderson and Cote (1998) found that high-recognition logos should be highly natural, harmonious, and moderately detailed. In contrast, low-investment logos (i.e., low recognition) should be less natural but very harmonious. Finally, logos aimed at conveying a strong professional image should be moderately detailed and natural.

Building on these findings, Miceli et al. (2014) investigated how visual complexity and conceptual complexity affect brand logo evaluations at varying exposure levels. The study reveals that visual complexity initially boosts logo attitudes but declines with repeated exposure, while conceptual complexity starts negatively and improves over time. These findings are supported by van der Lans et al. (2009), who, through a comprehensive cross-national survey, reported a consistent positive relationship between logo elaborateness and consumer attitudes. Similarly, van Grinsven and Das (2016) confirmed that visually complex logos generate more favorable consumer attitudes.

While several studies have analyzed design elements in terms of brand logos (e.g., Henderson & Cote, 1998; Miceli et al., 2014), advertisement effectiveness (e.g., Pieters et al., 2010), and package design (e.g.,

Baek et al., 2023; Favier et al., 2019), very few contributions have examined how design elements influence consumers' perceptions in eco-labels context (e.g., Donato & Adigüzel, 2022, 2024; Rihn et al., 2019; Tang et al., 2004). Importantly, no research to date—at least according to the available literature—has analyzed the role of eco-label design elements on sustainability perceptions. Therefore, the objective of this research is to investigate how eco-label visual design elements affect consumer sustainability perceptions and label adoption.

The proliferation of eco-labels worldwide reflects the growing demand for green certifications, but it also poses risks such as increased consumer confusion (Brécard, 2014; Moon et al., 2017) and difficulties in understanding their meaning (Rihn et al., 2019), which can undermine their effectiveness in signaling sustainability. Therefore, a well-crafted eco-label is essential for enhancing consumers' perceptions of sustainability and their adoption.

In that sense, the concept of visual complexity which refers to the extent of intricacy present within an image (Kaplan et al., 1972) is quite relevant, as it has been demonstrated to affect several viewers' perceptual responses, including the length of exposure and perceptual curiosity about objects (Sun & Firestone, 2021), and also influences consumers' understanding of a product or brand (Favier et al., 2019; Orth & Crouch, 2014), shaping their attitudes toward the target (e.g., Cox & Cox, 2002). For instance, Favier et al. (2019) found that complexity in package design leads to perceptions of sophistication and seduction, while simplicity is linked to sobriety, reliability, and authenticity. Baek et al. (2023) find that visually complex packaging positively influences evaluations of virtue products by enhancing hedonic utility.

The concept of conceptual complexity, which refers to the level of cognitive effort required to interpret and understand a design (Perussia, 1998), is equally important. Higher conceptual complexity often challenges viewers by presenting abstract or multifaceted ideas that require more cognitive processing (Lewis & Frank, 2016). This can enhance engagement and evoke deeper reflection, particularly in advertising, where visual metaphors play a critical role (Van Mulken et al., 2014). However, excessive complexity can hinder comprehension and reduce appeal, especially for unfamiliar designs (Miceli et al., 2014).

When these insights are applied to eco-label logos, it can be expected that consumers prefer eco-labels with high visual elaboration (i.e., high visual complexity) that are able to communicate clear, easily interpreted meanings (i.e., low conceptual complexity, see Donato & Adıgüzel, 2024). However, research has not yet clarified whether the same effects can be expected for eco-label logo perceived sustainability and adoption.

Despite previous studies suggesting that simplicity, often associated with minimalism, aligns with eco-conscious principles such as resource efficiency and essential functionality (e.g., Majer et al., 2022; Nickel & Böhm, 2024; Wang et al., 2024), in the case of visual stimuli with small dimensions—such as eco-label logos, which are often hard to notice on packaging—it can be expected that a design capable of capturing attention (i.e., visually complex) will also be effective in conveying its underlying sustainability message and to be adopted. In fact, eye-tracking studies (Guyader et al., 2017; Rihn et al., 2019; Song et al., 2019) underlined the importance of increasing eco-label visual attention, demonstrating that only once noted, eco-labels can positively affect consumer behavior. Coherently, it is possible to suppose that eco-label visual complexity positively affects consumers' sustainability perceptions and label adoption. Formally:

H_1: Visual complexity has a positive effect on (a) eco-label perceived sustainability and (b) eco-label adoption.

Conversely, the sustainability message conveyed by the label should be easy to process so that consumers are not only drawn to the label but also immediately understand its meaning. Stimuli that are easier to process tend to be perceived as more trustworthy, credible (Alter & Oppenheimer, 2009; Reber & Unkelbach, 2010; Schwarz, 2004), and authentic (Luffarelli et al., 2019). Therefore, it is reasonable to hypothesize that eco-label designs that convey their sustainable meaning immediately, exhibiting low levels of conceptual complexity, will be perceived as authentically more sustainable and will be more readily adopted.

H_2: Conceptual complexity has a negative effect on (a) eco-label perceived sustainability and (b) eco-label adoption.

Another key visual element that communicates sustainability is label color. The role of color in shaping sustainability perceptions is well-documented in the marketing literature. Pichierri and Pino (2023) examine how color saturation affects consumer perceptions of product sustainability, revealing that less saturated tones, such as pastels and earth hues, are often perceived as more eco-friendly than bright, highly satu-rated colors. This perception is linked to cultural associations with natural elements like soil, plants, and water, while bright colors are often asso-ciated with artificiality and industrial production, which can reduce a product's perceived environmental friendliness.

In general, green is frequently used by eco-label designers to enhance consumer recognition and evaluation, due to its strong conceptual connection with environmental issues (e.g., Pancer et al., 2017; Seo & Scammon, 2017; Sundar & Kellaris, 2015). Similarly, Hallez et al. (2023) note that colors like green and brown are strongly linked to sustainability, whereas red and yellow evoke perceptions of tastiness and indulgence.

Given the implicit association of green with environmental sustain-ability, it is possible to suppose that its use in eco-label design is likely to enhance perceived sustainability and eco-label adoption. Formally:

> H_3: The use of green color has a positive effect on (a) eco-label perceived sustainability and (b) eco-label adoption.

Each eco-label consists of both graphical elements (i.e., the logo) and textual components (i.e., label name, source, and sometimes information about its meaning). Therefore, it is essential to also consider the textual aspects of eco-labels.

Previous research (Rihn et al., 2019; Tang et al., 2004; Teisl et al., 2002) highlights that, although to a lesser extent, the textual components of eco-labels influence consumer perceptions. While marketing studies have shown that visual communication (such as images and logos) is generally more effective for memorization and recall than verbal commu-nication (i.e., texts and words; e.g., Lieberman & Culpepper, 1965), there are instances where this "picture dominance" does not apply. For example, written messages can be more effective when consumers are highly motivated and able to process the semantic content of the message (Childers & Houston, 1984).

According to Luffarelli et al. (2019), more descriptive logos facili-tate easier processing, as the textual elements they incorporate provide greater information about the marketed product. This is particularly rele-vant in the sustainable context. Similarly, it can be hypothesized that consumers will perceive eco-labels containing textual information as more sustainable and will be more willing to adopt them, as this information

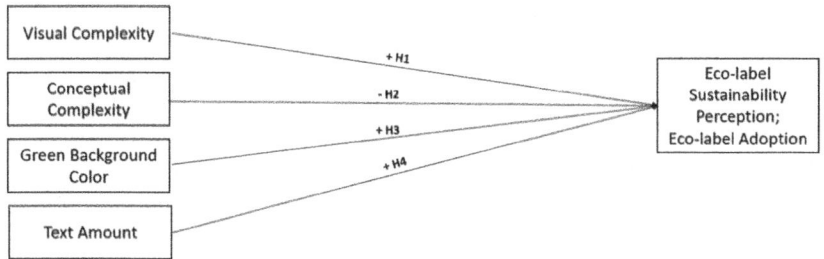

Fig. 1 Conceptual model

aids consumers in understanding the green nature of the certification. Formally:

H_4: Textual information has a positive effect on (a) eco-label perceived sustainability and (b) eco-label adoption.

Figure 1 summarizes the conceptual model tested in the study.

In the following section, a survey study designed to test the proposed hypotheses will be presented.

3   METHODOLOGY

The objective of the empirical study is threefold: first, to test the effect of eco-label design elements (i.e., visual and conceptual complexity, color, and textual information) on eco-label sustainability perceptions (H_{1a}-H_{4a}), second, to verify the effect of eco-label design on consumer responses, namely label adoption (H_{1b}-H_{4b}). Finally, this study wants to verify an additional measure of consumer evaluations toward eco-labels, namely perceived credibility, and describe eco-label recognition among the italian population.

3.1   Stimuli Selection[2]

A research assistant, unaware of the study's objectives, was tasked with observing the most frequently used Type I eco-labels in retail settings. This was based on an examination of products available on the websites of five Italian retailers, including two general supermarkets (i.e., https://www.conad.it/; and https://www.carrefour.it/), two discount stores (i.e., https://www.todis.it/ and https://www.lidl.it/), and one specialty store specializing in organic products (i.e., https://www.naturasi.it). On the basis of the observations on a wide array of various products, 15 Type I eco-labels were selected: five eco-labels that certify ecological production (i.e., EU eco-label, USDA eco-label, AB eco-label, JAS eco-label, SOIL eco-label), eight eco-labels that certify the environmental sustainability in terms of management of resources and production processes (i.e., ICEA eco-label, FSC eco-label, PEFC eco-label, RSPO eco-label, EMAS eco-label, ASC eco-label, MSC eco-label, Rainforest Alliance eco-label); and two eco-labels that certify Fair Trade (i.e., Fair Trade, WFTO). The selected labels were saved as a JPEG file (bitmaps of 250×250 pixels) after some adjustments in the paint program to put them in the same size (see Fig. 2).

3.2   Visual Dimensions Operationalization

Following the same procedures of Miceli et al. (2014), two pre-test studies were firstly conducted to measure the visual and conceptual complexity of selected eco-labels, allowing the use of these scores in the subsequent main study.

To prevent common method bias (Podsakoff et al., 2003) complexity scores were collected from two different samples.

Pre-test 1: Measuring visual complexity of selected eco-labels[3]

---

[2] The stimuli selected and the related scoring system utilized in this study have been previously adopted and validated in the following works: Donato & Adiguzel (2022) and Donato & Adiguzel (2024).

[3] All procedures performed in the study involving human participants were in accordance with the ethical standards of the institutional and/or national research committee and with the 1964 Helsinki declaration and its later amendments or comparable ethical standards. The identity of respondents was completely anonymous. Informed consensus was obtained from all individual participants included in the study.

Fig. 2   Selected stimuli

Four academics (3 males, 1 female; M_{age} = 40 years, SD = 8.91) were provided with the definition of visual complexity (i.e., the variety of visual information featured by a logo; Berlyne, 1970) and asked to independently assess the visual complexity of each of the 15 selected eco-labels on a seven-point Likert scale, with higher values indicating greater visual complexity. Reliability between experts was good (α = 0.83) indicating agreement between them. According to the given evaluations, WFTO and RAINFOREST were assessed as the most visually complex eco-labels, USDA and FSC were assessed as the least visually complex eco-labels (see Fig. 2).

Pre-test 2: Measuring conceptual complexity of selected eco-labels

Since conceptual complexity refers to the ability of a logo to evoke multiple meanings but not a consensually held one (Perussia, 1988), twenty-two undergraduate students (11 females, M_{age} = 22 years, SD = 1.56) listed up to ten meanings they associate with the proposed 15 eco-labels randomly shown. Then we computed an entropy score where the highest values indicate high conceptual complexity (Ellis et al., 1974; Henderson & Cote 1998), using the following formula:

$entropy = - \sum p_i In(p_i)$

The formula operates as follows: for instance, if 50% of respondents associate the eco-label with the word "green," 30% with "leave," and 20% with "nature," the entropy is calculated as $-[0.50 * (ln(0.50)) + 0.30 * (ln(0.30)) + 0.20 * (ln(0.20))]$, resulting in an entropy value of 1.03. The maximum entropy value of + 3 occurs when each of the 22 respondents provides a unique word for the eco-label (calculated as $-20 * 0.05 * (ln(0.05)) = -20 * (-0.15) = 3$). Conversely, the minimum entropy value of zero is reached if all 22 respondents use the same word for the eco-label (calculated as $-20 * 1 * (ln(1)) = 0$).

According to the results, SOIL and WFTO were the most conceptually complex, and PEFC and USDA were the least conceptually complex eco-labels among the 15 labels (see Table 1).

3.3   Color Background and Textual Information Operationalization

For eco-label color, since the elements that compose an eco-label, such as leaves, trees, fish, etc., might also create meanings (Elliot et al., 2007), affecting, therefore, conceptual complexity, we decided to focus

Table 1 Eco-labels and design elements' scores

Eco-label	Visual complexity Mean	Conceptual complexity Mean	Color Background	Textual Information
Organic EU	3.50	1.6334	Green	0
ASC	3.50	1.6118	Blue	5
WFTO	5.25	2.6094	White	4
JAS	3.25	2.1271	White	1
SOIL	4.25	2.6610	White	3
MSC	3.50	1.6872	Blue	5
EMAS	4.25	2.1582	White	1
PEFC	3.50	1.0048	White	2
RAIN	5.00	2.0636	White	5
USDA	2.00	1.5237	White	2
FAIR TRADE	3.50	2.4314	Black	2
AB	3.00	1.7342	Green	3
RSPO	3.25	2.1827	White	7
FSC	2.50	1.6426	Green	10
ICEA	4.25	2.3402	White	5

on eco-label background color, also because it is the design part that takes the most space on the label. Moreover, according to Celhay and Luffarelli (2024), color of a logo's background is a physical, contextual cue that shapes the meaning evoked by the hue of the positive space. Green, blue, and black were compared against white which was the most popular choice for background among 15 eco-labels. Textual information was operationalized by counting the number of words contained in each eco-label (i.e., text size). Conceptual and visual complexity, textual information, and color background measures of selected eco-labels were reported in Table 1.

3.4   Procedure

Data was collected through a Qualtrics online survey from 460 Italian undergraduate and graduate students from a large Italian University ($M_{\mathrm{age}} = 25.68$ years, $SD = 8.92$, 50.2% females) recruited via email.

In particular, participants were informed that they would be evaluating a series of logos, without being explicitly told that the logos were related to eco-labels. Each participant was then exposed, in random order, to the 15 selected eco-labels and asked to indicate the following for each: whether they recognized the label (eco-label recognition: YES/NO), their perception of the label's sustainability (eco-label perceived sustainability: two items on a seven-point Likert scale, "Products with this label are environmentally friendly" and "Products with this label are sustainable" ($\alpha = 0.88$)) and the extent to which they considered the label in their purchasing decisions (eco-label adoption: seven-point Likert scale, "To what extent do you take this label into account when you shop?").

As an additional exploratory variable, participants also reported their perception of the eco-label's credibility (eco-label perceived credibility: two items on a seven-point Likert scale, "Firms producing products with this label are reputable," and "I trust firms producing products with this label"; Adıgüzel & Donato, 2021, $\alpha = 0.91$).

Environmental concern was measured using a six-item scale (Haws et al., 2014; $\alpha = 0.91$; $M = 4.84$, $SD = 1.03$; see Table 2). Finally, participants provided demographic information, such as age and gender.

4   Results

In order to describe consumers' perceptions and awareness of eco-labels descriptive statistics for each measured variables were checked.

Eco-label recognition appears to be quite low, except for FSC, organic EU, MSC, and WFTO which got a recognition percentage above the 50% of the sample. Accordingly, the adoption of eco-labels is low ($M = 2.39$, $SD = 1.84$). JAS, SOIL, and EMAS are the least recognized labels, ASC and MSC are the most adopted eco-labels in purchase situations, opposite of JAS (see Table 3).

Given that all participants evaluated the same set of 15 eco-labels, two multilevel regression models were conducted using STATA 14 to test the conceptual model. Standardized scores of the variables were applied to facilitate the interpretation of effect magnitudes. The independent variables included visual and conceptual complexity, textual information, and color dummies (green, blue, black vs. white), measured according to the pre-tests and operationalization described earlier. The dependent variables were eco-label perceived sustainability and eco-label adoption. Age, gender, label recognition, and environmental concerns were included as control variables.

Testing H_{1a}-H_{4a}:   Label   Perceived   Sustainability.   While   visual complexity had a positive effect on label perceived sustainability ($b =$

Table 2 Measurement items

Scale and Source	Item and Reliability
Perceived Sustainability Adıgüzel and Donato (2021)	The products with this label on are environmentally friendly The products with this label on are sustainable ($\alpha = 0.90$)
Eco-label Adoption Thøgersen et al. (2010)	To what extent do you take this label into account when you shop? 1 = Never, 7 = Always
Environmental Concern Haws et al. (2014)	I consider the potential environmental impact of my actions when making many of my decisions My purchase habits are affected by my concern for our environment I am concerned about wasting the resources of our planet I would describe myself as environmentally responsible I am willing to be inconvenienced in order to take actions that are more environmentally friendly $\alpha = 0.91$
Eco-label recognition Self-made	Do you recognize this label? YES/NO
Eco-label Perceived Credibility Adıgüzel and Donato (2021)	Firms that produce products with this label are very reputable, I trust firms produce products with this label ($\alpha = 0.91$)

0.032, $p < 0.01$), conceptual complexity had a negative effect ($b = -0.054$, $p < 0.001$). Moreover, perceived sustainability ($b = 0.170$, $p < 0.001$) was higher for eco-labels with green color background compared to white ones. Textual information had also a positive effect on product sustainability.

Regarding the control variables, eco-label perceived sustainability ($b = 0.397$, $p < 0.001$) was higher when consumers recognized the eco-label, and when age increased, eco-label perceived sustainability ($b = -0.183$, $p < 0.001$) decreased. Finally, environmental concern had a positive effect on perceived sustainability ($b = 0.181$, $p < 0.001$).

Table 3 Descriptives

Eco-label	Eco-label Adoption Mean (SD)	Recognition Yes%	Perceived Sustainability Mean (SD)	Perceived Reliability Mean (SD)
Organic EU	2.72 (1.90)	65.22	4.64 (1.51)	4.33 (1.44)
ICEA	2.49 (1.74)	36.74	4.78 (1.42)	4.50 (1.39)
FSC	2.70 (1.85)	73.91	4.79 (1.47)	4.38 (1.41)
RSPO	2.21 (1.61)	27.83	4.41 (1.46)	4.04 (1.39)
AB	2.60 (1.70)	48.48	4.97 (1.36)	4.62 (1.29)
Fair Trade	2.49 (1.89)	45.00	3.96 (1.50)	4.12 (1.53)
USDA	1.77 (1.33)	18.91	4.22 (1.42)	3.82 (1.34)
RAINFOREST	2.21 (1.66)	35.43	4.76 (1.45)	4.32 (1.38)
PEFC	1.92 (1.38)	31.30	4.36 (1.48)	3.64 (1.33)
EMAS	1.61 (1.15)	16.74	3.66 (1.35)	3.56 (1.29)
MSC	3.00 (1.92)	61.30	4.95 (1.40)	4.70 (1.36)
SOIL	1.75 (1.29)	15.00	4.21 (1.45)	3.88 (1.33)
JAS	1.54 (1.11)	8.26	3.93 (1.33)	3.63 (1.23)
WFTO	2.42 (1.75)	53.04	4.12 (1.39)	4.40 (1.45)
ASC	4.41 (2.66)	45.43	4.66 (1.41)	4.52 (1.35)

These results confirm the proposed conceptualization, according to which eco-labels presenting higher visual complexity (H_{1a}), low conceptual complexity (H_{2a}), with green background (H_{3a}), and presenting textual information (H4a) are perceived as more sustainable.

Testing H_{1b}-H_{4b}: Adoption of Eco-Label. A second multilevel regression model, with eco-label adoption as the dependent variable, was conducted. The results revealed that, in line with H_{1b}, visual complexity had a positive effect on label adoption ($b = 0.103$, $p < 0.001$). However, the effect of conceptual complexity was positive but not significant (b = 0.009, p = 0.81). Labels with green (b = 0.449, p < 0.001), blue (b = 1.347, p < 0.001), and black backgrounds (b = 0.491, p < 0.001) were adopted more frequently by consumers compared to those with a white background. Additionally, consumers were more likely to adopt labels that contained more textual information (b = 0.110, p < 0.001).

Interestingly, adoption increased when age (b = 0.176, p < 0.001), environmental concern (b = 0.466, p < 0.001), and label recognition (b = 2.378, p < 0.001) increased.

Moreover, when label recognition was not included in the model, the effect of conceptual complexity was negative and significant, as hypothe-sized in H$_{2b}$ (b =−0.116, p < 0.01). This finding is consistent with the results of Miceli et al. (2014), which indicated that conceptually complex visual stimuli are negatively perceived by consumers. However, this effect becomes positive as consumers become familiar with (i.e., recognize) the stimulus.

Explorative Variable: Eco-Label Credibility. An additional exploratory multilevel regression was conducted, considering consumers' perception of label credibility as the dependent variable. While previous research has shown that angular shapes are perceived as more reliable than rounded shapes (e.g., Jiang et al., 2016), no prior research has explored the extent to which visual dimensions—such as visual and conceptual complexity, background color, and the amount of textual information—communi-cate credibility, particularly in the context of green consumption, where sustainability is considered a credence good. In this regard, the present empirical work could serve as a foundation for future research in this domain.

The results revealed that while visual complexity had a positive effect on consumer perceptions of label credibility (b = 0.072, p < 0.001), conceptual complexity had a negative effect (b = −0.003, p < 0.05). Perceived credibility was higher for eco-labels with a green (b = 0.194, p < 0.001) and a blue (b = 0.261, p < 0.001) background compared to white ones. Labels having black background do not affect credibility perceptions (b = 0.056, p ns).

Textual information also had a positive effect on credibility percep-tions (b = 0.056, p < 0.001). Regarding the control variables, labels recognized are perceived as more credible (b = 0.470, p < 0.001), more-over, environmental concern positively affected credibility perceptions (b = 0.210, p < 0.001). Coherently with previous analyses as age increased,

Table 4   Results of multilevel regression models (standardized coefficients)

	Label Sustainability Perceptions	Eco-label Adoption	Label Credibility Perceptions
Visual complexity	0.032**	0.103***	0.072***
Conceptual complexity	−0.054***	0.009	−0.003*
Text Amount	0.079 ***	0.110***	0.056***
Background: Green	0.170***	0.449***	0.194***
Background: Blue	0.167***	1.347***	0.261***
Background: Black	−0.185***	0.491***	0.056
Background: White			
Eco-label recognition	0.397***	2.378***	0.470***
Environmental concern	0.181***	0.466***	0.210***
Age	−0.183***	0.176***	−0.156***
Female (1)	−0.084	−0.214	−0.087
Wald	1086.33 ***	1883.56***	1163.78 ***

Notes * $p < 0.05$ ** $p < 0.01$ *** $p < 0.001$

consumer label credibility label decreased ($b = -0.156$, $p < 0.001$). Table 4 summarizes the results of the study.

5   DISCUSSION

The study presents an analysis of consumers' perceptions, awareness, and adoption of existing eco-labels, investigating the influence of the visual dimensions of eco-label logos on both perceived sustainability and label adoption. Through multilevel regression models, the research delves into the visual, conceptual, and textual attributes of eco-label logos and their effects on consumer behavior. In particular, it investigates how visual complexity, conceptual complexity, background color, and textual information affect eco-label sustainability perception and adoption, while considering control variables such as age, gender, and environmental concern.

The first multilevel regression model tested the effects of visual complexity, conceptual complexity, background color, and textual information on *perceived sustainability*. The results revealed several important findings that align with the hypotheses.

Visual Complexity. One of the most notable outcomes was the positive effect of visual complexity on perceived sustainability. The positive relationship suggests that eco-labels with more elaborate designs may convey a sense of environmental care, which could reinforce the idea of sustainability. This result is partially consistent with prior research. Despite the association between simplicity and sustainability, extensive logo research (e.g., Miceli et al., 2014; van der Lans et al., 2009) shows that logos with higher visual elaboration foster more favorable attitudes by attracting attention and stimulating curiosity. This relationship appears to hold true within the sustainability domain as well.

Conceptual Complexity. In contrast, conceptual complexity had a negative impact on perceived sustainability. Conceptual complexity refers to how difficult it is for consumers to understand the meaning or purpose of the label (Donato & Adıgüzel, 2024). If a label's messaging or symbolism is unclear, it can undermine consumers' perceptions of the label's authenticity. This result suggests that eco-labels should aim for clear and straightforward communication to foster perceptions of sustainability. Prior research, such as the study by Miceli et al. (2014), supports this notion by indicating that conceptually complex visual stimuli are often negatively perceived by consumers, as they may require more cognitive effort to process.

Green Background Color. The study also revealed that background color plays a significant role in shaping consumers' perceptions of eco-labels. Eco-labels with green backgrounds were perceived as significantly more sustainable than those with white backgrounds. This finding aligns with common associations between the color green and environmental consciousness, as green is often linked to nature and sustainability (Labrecque & Milne, 2012). Interestingly, eco-labels with blue backgrounds also enhanced perceived sustainability, corroborating findings from previous research (Pichierri & Pino, 2023). This suggests that blue, often associated with water and cleanliness, may also evoke feelings of environmental stewardship. Contrary to the findings of Celhay and Luffarelli (2024), white backgrounds were not found to be effective in the context of eco-labels.

Textual Information. Furthermore, textual information on eco-labels was found to have a positive impact on perceived sustainability. Consumers tend to perceive eco-labels with descriptive information as more trustworthy and credible, possibly because they offer concrete details about the product's environmental benefits. This aligns with research that emphasizes the role of transparency and information in shaping consumer trust, especially in markets where sustainability is a credence attribute, meaning its authenticity cannot be easily verified by consumers themselves (Donato & Adıgüzel, 2024).

Control Variables. The control variables provided additional insights into how demographic and psychographic factors influence eco-label perceptions. Label recognition was a strong predictor of perceived sustainability, confirming that familiarity with a label enhances consumers' trust and perception of its sustainability. Additionally, age had a negative relationship with perceived sustainability, indicating that older consumers may be more skeptical of eco-labels. Finally, environmental concern positively influenced perceived sustainability, demonstrating that consumers with higher environmental consciousness are more likely to perceive eco-labels as sustainable.

The second multilevel regression model focused on *eco-label adoption*, exploring the factors that drive consumers to choose eco-labeled products. Similar to perceived sustainability, several label visual characteristics were found to have significant effects on adoption.

Visual Complexity. The results confirmed that visual complexity positively affects eco-label adoption. This indicates that consumers are more likely to adopt eco-labeled products when the labels have visually sophisticated designs. This finding is consistent with the idea that visually complex labels may attract attention (e.g., Miceli et al., 2024), making consumers more likely to choose these products.

Conceptual Complexity. Unlike in the perceived sustainability model, the effect of conceptual complexity on adoption was positive but not significant when label recognition was included as a variable. However, when label recognition was excluded from the model, conceptual complexity had a negative and significant effect on adoption. This suggests that conceptual complexity hinders adoption when consumers are unfamiliar with the label, but as they become more familiar, the negative effect diminishes. This pattern reinforces the importance of clear and easily interpretable labels for consumers, especially when they are unfamiliar with the brand or certification.

Green Background Color. Background color also played a crucial role in label adoption. Eco-labels with green, blue, and black backgrounds were adopted more frequently than those with white backgrounds. This finding further emphasizes the significance of color in conveying sustainability cues. The strong effect of blue backgrounds on adoption is particularly interesting, as it suggests that consumers may associate blue with environmental benefits beyond the typical connotations of green, such as water conservation or cleanliness.

Textual Information. As with perceived sustainability, textual information had a positive effect on eco-label adoption. This finding highlights the importance of providing clear, informative content on eco-labels to encourage consumer adoption (Donato & D'Aniello, 2022). Consumers are more likely to trust and choose products when they feel informed about the product's environmental benefits.

Control Variables. The control variables revealed that age, environmental concern, and label recognition all had positive effects on eco-label adoption. These results suggest that older consumers, environmentally conscious individuals, and those who recognize the eco-label are more likely to adopt eco-labeled products. The strong effect of label recognition underscores the importance of brand and label familiarity in driving consumer choices.

The results of an additional exploratory analysis considering consumers' perceptions of eco-label credibility revealed that visual complexity positively affects label credibility, while conceptual complexity negatively affects it. These findings align with the sustainability and adoption models, suggesting that visually intricate but conceptually clear labels are perceived as more credible. Furthermore, eco-labels with green and blue backgrounds were perceived as more credible than those with white backgrounds, while black backgrounds had no significant effect on credibility. Textual information also positively influenced credibility perceptions, confirming that providing detailed information enhances consumer trust in eco-labels.

References

Adıgüzel, F., & Donato, C. (2021). Proud to be sustainable: Upcycled versus recycled luxury products. *Journal of Business Research, 130*, 137–146.

Alter, A. L., & Oppenheimer, D. M. (2009). Uniting the tribes of fluency to form a metacognitive nation. *Personality and Social Psychology Review, 13*(3), 219–235.

Atkinson, L., & Rosenthal, S. (2014). Signaling the green sell: The influence of eco-label source, argument specificity, and product involvement on consumer trust. *Journal of Advertising, 43*(1), 33–45.

Baek, E., Huang, Z., & Lee, S. S. (2023). Visual complexity= hedonic? Effects of visually complex packages on consumer perceptions and evaluations of products. *Journal of Retailing and Consumer Services, 74*, 103435.

Berlyne, D. E. (1970). Novelty, complexity and hedonic value. *Perception and Psychophysics, 8*, 279–286.

Brécard, D. (2014). Consumer confusion over the profusion of eco-labels: Lessons from a double differentiation model. *Resource and Energy Economics, 37*, 64–84.

Celhay, F., & Luffarelli, J. (2024). Competent or sad blue? Lively or aggressive red? Why, how, and when background color shapes the meanings of logo hues. *Journal of Consumer Research, 51*(4), ucae019

Childers, T. L., & Houston, M. J. (1984). Conditions for a picture-superiority effect on consumer memory. *Journal of Consumer Research, 11*(2), 643–654.

Cox, D., & Cox, A. D. (2002). Beyond first impressions: The effects of repeated exposure on consumer liking of visually complex and simple product designs. *Journal of the Academy of Marketing Science, 30*(2), 119–130.

Dijksterhuis, A., Smith, P. K., Van Baaren, R. B., & Wigboldus, D. H. (2005). The unconscious consumer: Effects of environment on consumer behavior. *Journal of Consumer Psychology, 15*(3), 193–202.

Donato, C., & Adıgüzel, F. (2022). Visual complexity of eco-labels and product evaluations in online setting: Is simple always better? *Journal of Retailing and Consumer Services, 67*, 102961.

Donato, C., & Adıgüzel, F. (2024). The effects of visual design on eco-labels evaluations: Guidelines for effective green advertising. *Journal of Marketing Theory and Practice*, 1–18.

Donato, C., Barone, A. M., & Romani, S. (2021). The satiating power of sustainability: The effect of package sustainability on perceived satiation of healthy food. *British Food Journal, 123*(13), 162–177.

Donato, C., & D'Aniello, A. (2022). Tell me more and make me feel proud: The role of eco-labels and informational cues on consumers' food perceptions. *British Food Journal, 124*(4), 1365–1382.

Eldesouky, A., Mesias, F. J., & Escribano, M. (2020). Perception of Spanish consumers towards environmentally friendly labelling in food. *International Journal of Consumer Studies, 44*(1), 64–76.

Elliot, A. J., Maier, M. A., Moller, A. C., Friedman, R., & Meinhardt, J. (2007). Color and psychological functioning: The effect of red on performance attainment. *Journal of Experimental Psychology, 136*, 154–168.

Ellis, H. C., Parente, F. J., & Shumate, E. C. (1974). Meaningfulness, perceptual grouping, and organization in recognition memory. *Journal of Experimental Psychology, 102*(2), 308.

Favier, M., Celhay, F., & Pantin-Sohier, G. (2019). Is less more or a bore? Package design simplicity and brand perception: An application to Champagne. *Journal of Retailing and Consumer Services, 46*, 11–20.

Gallopín, G., Jiménez Herrero, L. M., & Rocuts, A. (2014). Conceptual frameworks and visual interpretations of sustainability. *International Journal of Sustainable Development, 17*(3), 298–326.

Grunert, K. G., Hieke, S., & Wills, J. (2014). Sustainability labels on food products: Consumer motivation, understanding and use. *Food Policy, 44*, 177–189.

Guyader, H., Ottosson, M., & Witell, L. (2017). You can't buy what you can't see: Retailer practices to increase the green premium. *Journal of Retailing and Consumer Services, 34*, 319–325.

Hallez, L., Vansteenbeeck, H., Boen, F., & Smits, T. (2023). Persuasive packaging? The impact of packaging color and claims on young consumers' perceptions of product healthiness, sustainability and tastiness. *Appetite, 182*, 106433.

Haws, K. L., Winterich, K. P., & Naylor, R. W. (2014). Seeing the world through GREEN-tinted glasses: Green consumption values and responses to environmentally friendly products. *Journal of Consumer Psychology, 24*(3), 336–354.

Henderson, P. W., & Cote, J. A. (1998). Guidelines for selecting or modifying logos. *Journal of Marketing, 62*(2), 14–30.

Jiang, Y., Gorn, G. J., Galli, M., & Chattopadhyay, A. (2016). Does your company have the right logo? How and why circular-and angular-logo shapes influence brand attribute judgments. *Journal of Consumer Research, 42*(5), 709–726.

Ji, S., & Lin, P. S. (2022). Aesthetics of sustainability: Research on the design strategies for emotionally durable visual communication design. *Sustainability, 14*(8), 4649.

Kaplan, S., Kaplan, R., & Wendt, J. S. (1972). Rated preference and complexity for natural and urban visual material. *Perception & Psychophysics, 12*(4), 354–356.

Labrecque, L. I., & Milne, G. R. (2012). Exciting red and competent blue: The importance of color in marketing. *Journal of the Academy of Marketing Science, 40*(5), 711–727.

Lewis, M. L., & Frank, M. C. (2016). The length of words reflects their conceptual complexity. *Cognition, 153,* 182–195.

Lieberman, L. R., & Culpepper, J. T. (1965). Words versus objects: Comparison of free verbal recall. *Psychological Reports, 17*(3), 983–988.

Luffarelli, J., Mukesh, M., & Mahmood, A. (2019). Let the logo do the talking: The influence of logo descriptiveness on brand equity. *Journal of Marketing Research, 56*(5), 862–878.

Magnier, L., Schoormans, J., & Mugge, R. (2016). Judging a product by its cover: Packaging sustainability and perceptions of quality in food products. *Food Quality and Preference, 53,* 132–142.

Majer, J. M., Henscher, H. A., Reuber, P., Fischer-Kreer, D., & Fischer, D. (2022). The effects of visual sustainability labels on consumer perception and behavior: A systematic review of the empirical literature. *Sustainable Production and Consumption, 33,* 1–14.

Meyerding, S. G., & Merz, N. (2018). Consumer preferences for organic labels in Germany using the example of apples–combining choice-based conjoint analysis and eye-tracking measurements. *Journal of Cleaner Production, 181,* 772–783.

Miceli, G. N., Scopelliti, I., Raimondo, M. A., & Donato, C. (2014). Breaking through complexity: Visual and conceptual dimensions in logo evaluation across exposures. *Psychology & Marketing, 31*(10), 886–899.

Moon, S. J., Costello, J. P., & Koo, D. M. (2017). The impact of consumer confusion from eco-labels on negative WOM, distrust, and dissatisfaction. *International Journal of Advertising, 36*(2), 246–271.

Ní Choisdealbha, Á., & Lunn, P. D. (2020). Green and simple: Disclosures on eco-labels interact with situational constraints in consumer choice. *Journal of Consumer Policy, 43*(4), 699–722.

Nickel, K., & Böhm, R. A. (2024). Power versus morality: Uncovering the underlying mechanisms of consumer response to perceived visual sustainability in package design. *Journal of Product & Brand Management.*

Orth, U. R., & Crouch, R. C. (2014). Is beauty in the aisles of the retailer? Package processing in visually complex contexts. *Journal of Retailing, 90*(4), 524–537.

Pancer, E., McShane, L., & Noseworthy, T. J. (2017). Isolated environmental cues and product efficacy penalties: The color green and eco-labels. *Journal of Business Ethics, 143*(1), 159–177.

Perussia, F. (1988). Semiotic frame: A method for the experimental analysis of images. *Psychological Reports, 63,* 524–526.

Pichierri, M., & Pino, G. (2023). Less saturated, more eco-friendly: Color saturation and consumer perception of product sustainability. *Psychology & Marketing, 40*(9), 1830–1849.

Pieters, R., Wedel, M., & Batra, R. (2010). The stopping power of advertising: Measures and effects of visual complexity. *Journal of Marketing, 74*(5), 48–60.

Podsakoff, P. M., MacKenzie, S. B., Lee, J. Y., & Podsakoff, N. P. (2003). Common method biases in behavioral research: A critical review of the literature and recommended remedies. *Journal of Applied Psychology, 88*(5), 879.

Reber, R., & Unkelbach, C. (2010). The epistemic status of processing fluency as source for judgments of truth. *Review of Philosophy and Psychology, 1*(4), 563–581.

Rihn, A., Wei, X., & Khachatryan, H. (2019). Text vs. logo: Does eco-label format influence consumers' visual attention and willingness-to-pay for fruit plants? An experimental auction approach. *Journal of Behavioral and Experimental Economics, 82*, 101452.

Schwarz, N. (2004). Metacognitive experiences in consumer judgment and decision making. *Journal of Consumer Psychology, 14*(4), 332–348.

Seo, J. Y., & Scammon, D. L. (2017). Do green packages lead to misperceptions? The influence of package colours on consumers' perceptions of brands with environmental claims. *Marketing Letters, 28*(3), 357–369.

Song, L., Lim, Y., Chang, P., Guo, Y., Zhang, M., Wang, X., ... & Cai, H. (2019). Ecolabel's role in informing sustainable consumption: A naturalistic decision making study using eye tracking glasses. *Journal of cleaner production, 218*, 685–695.

Sun, Z., & Firestone, C. (2021). Curious objects: How visual complexity guides attention and engagement. *Cognitive Science, 45*(4), e12933.

Sundar, A., & Kellaris, J. J. (2015). Blue-washing the green halo. *The psychology of design: Creating Consumer Appeal*, 63–74.

Tang, E., Fryxell, G. E., & Chow, C. S. (2004). Visual and verbal communication in the design of eco-label for green consumer products. *Journal of International Consumer Marketing, 16*(4), 85–105.

Teisl, M. F., Peavey, S., Newman, F., Buono, J., & Hermann, M. (2002). Consumer reactions to environmental labels for forest products: A preliminary look. *Forest Products Journal, 52*(1), 44.

Thøgersen, J., Haugaard, P., & Olesen, A. (2010). Consumer responses to ecolabels. *European Journal of Marketing, 44*(11/12), 1787–1810.

van der Lans, R., Cote, J. A., Cole, C. A., Leong, S. M., Smidts, A., Henderson, P. W., et al. (2009). Cross-national logo evaluation analysis: An individual-level approach. *Marketing Science, 28*, 968–985.

Van Grinsven, B., & Das, E. (2016). Logo design in marketing communications: Brand logo complexity moderates exposure effects on brand recognition and brand attitude. *Journal of Marketing Communications, 22*(3), 256–270.

Van Mulken, M., Van Hooft, A., & Nederstigt, U. (2014). Finding the tipping point: Visual metaphor and conceptual complexity in advertising. *Journal of Advertising, 43*(4), 333–343.

Wang, X., Chen, J., Ma, C., & Jiang, Y. (2024). Simpler is greener: The impact of packaging visual complexity on products' eco-friendliness perception. *Psychology & Marketing.*

Xin, Y., & Long, D. (2023). Linking eco-label knowledge and sustainable consumption of renewable energy: A roadmap towards green revolution. *Renewable Energy, 207,* 531–538.

CHAPTER 5

Implications for Academics, Practitioners, and Policymakers

Abstract This chapter discusses the implications of this book for academics, practitioners, and policymakers. By systematically analyzing eco-label perceptions and aesthetic dimensions, the book enriches academic discourse by merging aesthetic theory with green marketing. The empirical findings challenge conventional views on simplicity, demonstrating that visual complexity can enhance perceived sustainability. Marketers are advised to use green and blue backgrounds in eco-label designs and provide transparent textual information to build consumer trust. Retailers should prioritize eco-labeled products, while policymakers must establish clear standards and invest in public awareness campaigns to educate consumers, promoting sustainable consumption and a more environmentally conscious marketplace. Finally, the chapter underscores limitations and outlines avenues for further research.

Keywords Eco-labels · Aesthetic dimensions · Sustainable consumption · Consumer perceptions · Policymakers

1   INTRODUCTION

The central theme of the present book revolves around the growing importance of eco-label logos as essential tools for sustainable communication. In an era where consumers are inundated with countless choices across various product categories, eco-labels serve a critical role in helping individuals navigate this complexity. As discussed in Chapter 2, they provide a clear and concise indication of the environmental and ethical standards associated with a product, thus simplifying the decision-making process for consumers who prioritize sustainability.

However, the effective communication of sustainable choices through eco-labels presents numerous challenges. As highlighted in the literature (e.g., Donato & D'Aniello, 2022; Eldesouky et al., 2020; Grunert et al., 2014; Meyerding & Merz, 2018; Song et al., 2019), a significant portion of consumers remains unaware of the specific meanings and criteria behind various eco-labels. This lack of understanding can lead to confusion regarding the credibility and implications of the labels, ultimately diminishing their intended impact. The existing gap in consumer knowledge suggests a pressing need for ongoing education initiatives aimed at improving eco-label recognition and comprehension.

Regarding the latter point, given the crucial function of eco-labels in promoting sustainable consumption, it becomes especially important to understand the visual elements that enhance their communicative effectiveness. As examined in Chapter 3, aesthetic and visual dimensions play a pivotal role in influencing individuals' evaluations, particularly in the marketing domain. Therefore, visual design is crucial in shaping how consumers interpret eco-labels. Factors such as visual and conceptual complexity, color, and textual information can significantly impact consumer perceptions and behaviors toward eco-labeled products.

Eco-label literature has primarily focused on areas such as trust, credibility, and third-party certifications (Atkinson & Rosenthal, 2014; Teisl et al., 2008; Thøgersen, 2000), as well as comparisons between eco-labels and other signaling cues like sustainability tags, nutritional labels, or origin labels (Dekhili & Akli Achabou, 2014; Sigurdsson et al., 2022; Sirieix et al., 2013). Additionally, research has explored the sales outcomes associated with eco-labels (Teisl et al., 2002) and the consumer-specific factors influencing the use of eco-labels in decision-making, such as environmental concern, belief in responsible purchasing behavior, and general environmental orientation (Bickart & Ruth, 2012; Gaspar Ferreira & Fernandes, 2022; Thøgersen, 2000).

Limited research, however, has examined the influence of eco-label logos on consumer behavior, with notable exceptions in studies by Tang et al. (2004) and recent works by Donato and Adıgüzel (2022, 2024). However, these studies predominantly focus on consumers' attitudes toward the label or the labeled product, without addressing a more critical factor that underlies the effectiveness of eco-labels and sustainable logos in general: perceived sustainability.

The empirical study presented in Chapter 4 is, to the author's knowledge, the first systematic attempt to explore how eco-label design elements influence consumers' sustainability perceptions and label adoption. Additionally, the study examined the effects of eco-label design on perceived credibility. It focused on a key collative variable from Berlyne's (1970) framework—complexity, both visual and conceptual. In line with Donato and Adıgüzel's (2024) work, and considering the role of eco-labels as green certifications, two further visual design elements were analyzed: color, particularly sustainability-related hues, and the presence of textual information.

The findings from a survey conducted among 460 undergraduate and graduate students from a large Italian university, using 15 real eco-labels, reveal that visual complexity positively impacts both perceived sustainability and eco-label adoption, suggesting that intricate designs convey a sense of environmental care. Conversely, conceptual complexity negatively affects perceived sustainability and impedes adoption when label recognition is low, highlighting the importance of clear and straightforward label designs. Background color plays a crucial role, with green and blue eco-labels being perceived as more sustainable and leading to higher adoption intentions. Additionally, textual information enhances perceptions of sustainability and adoption by fostering transparency and trust. Control variables show that label recognition, environmental concern, and age influence consumer perceptions, with familiar eco-labels and higher environmental consciousness increasing adoption, while older consumers tend to be more skeptical. Lastly, visual complexity positively impacts perceived label credibility, whereas conceptual complexity has a negative effect, highlighting the importance of visually engaging and conceptually clear designs in building trust and promoting adoption.

2   IMPLICATIONS FOR ACADEMICS

Firstly, the present book offers a systematic analysis of the literature related to eco-label perceptions and the aesthetic dimensions in consumer research. More importantly, by bridging concepts from aesthetic theory and green marketing, the empirical study enriches the academic discourse on how visual and conceptual complexity, color schemes, and textual information in eco-labels affect consumer sustainability perceptions and adoption.

The first theoretical contribution of this empirical study lies in its assessment of how aesthetic variables influence consumer behavior in sustainability contexts. Traditionally, aesthetic theory has focused on the role of visual appeal in product design (e.g., Bloch, 1995; Veryzer & Hutchinson, 1998), or logo evaluation (e.g., Henderson & Cote, 1998; Miceli et al., 2014), often emphasizing how beauty, proportion, and balance can drive consumer preferences. This research extends that framework to include eco-labels, positioning them as not just functional markers of sustainability but also as aesthetic objects that must balance visual complexity and simplicity to achieve their intended goals.

The finding that visual complexity positively influences perceived sustainability and label adoption is particularly noteworthy. It challenges much of the existing literature, which has often emphasized that simplicity in design aligns better with sustainability principles, especially because minimalist designs are frequently associated with resource efficiency and functional clarity (e.g., Majer et al., 2022; Nickel & Böhm, 2024; Wang et al., 2024).

However, this research indicates that logos featuring elaborate and intricate designs are not only more likely to be adopted (Donato & Adıgüzel, 2024), but also effectively signal greater environmental responsibility to consumers. This finding is novel because it highlights how visual complexity—rather than simplicity—can be instrumental in shaping sustainability perceptions. The ability of complex designs to capture attention and stimulate curiosity seems to foster a more positive engagement with eco-labels, suggesting that rich visual stimuli play a critical role in the initial stages of consumer interaction.

Moreover, the results suggest that visual complexity enhances label credibility, extending findings on visual shape and product perceptions (e.g., Jiang et al., 2016). This aligns with prior research in the realm of product packaging, which has demonstrated that intricate designs can enhance consumer perceptions of quality (Creusen & Schoormans, 2005). In the context of logo design, Miceli et al. (2014) found that visually complex stimuli foster higher perceptual fluency, subsequently leading to more favorable attitudes toward the product. This additional role of visual complexity merits further exploration in other contexts related to sustainability.

Importantly, by applying these insights to eco-labels, this research expands the scope of aesthetic theory to include sustainable marketing, offering a new perspective on how visual design can function as a credibility signal in green marketing.

This research also reveals that the effect of complexity is not linear. While visual complexity enhances perceived sustainability, conceptual complexity—the difficulty of understanding a label's meaning—can have the opposite effect. This nuance highlights and confirms the dual role of complexity articulated by Berlyne (1970): while it can attract attention and signal quality, it must be balanced with clarity and simplicity to avoid overwhelming consumers. This aligns with prior research in cognitive psychology (Zajonc, 1968) and logo evaluation (Miceli et al., 2014), which has shown that overly complex designs can increase cognitive load, leading to negative evaluations. Moreover, results reveal that conceptual complexity negatively impacts perceived sustainability when label recognition is low; however, this effect diminishes as consumers become familiar with the label. This suggests that familiarity with certain eco-labels enhances consumers' ability to process and trust more complex messages. This dynamic aligns with the mere exposure effect, which posits that repeated exposure to a stimulus increases familiarity and, consequently, positive evaluations (Bornstein, 1989; Zajonc, 1968). Thus, marketing efforts aimed at building eco-label awareness and familiarity could mitigate the negative effects of conceptual complexity through repeated exposures, paving the way for further research into how marketing strategies can enhance consumer perceptions of sustainability. Another theoretical contribution pertains to color psychology research (e.g., Labrecque & Milne, 2012; Labrecque et al., 2013; Mai et al., 2016). Labels with green or blue backgrounds were perceived as more sustainable than those with white backgrounds, aligning with findings by Sundar and Kellaris (2017). Green is commonly associated with nature and environmental consciousness, while blue evokes feelings of water, cleanliness, and purity (Labrecque & Milne, 2012). These colors strengthen well-established associations in consumers' minds, thereby reinforcing the environmental message of the label. This insight contributes to the theoretical understanding of how color can be strategically utilized in eco-label design to enhance consumers' evaluations of sustainability claims.

Additionally, eco-labels featuring green, blue, and black backgrounds are perceived as more credible than those with white backgrounds. This result supports previous research indicating that green logos promote perceptions of ethicality and eco-friendliness (Lim et al., 2020; Sundar & Kellaris, 2017). Furthermore, Seo and Scammon (2017) found that the use of green in product packaging enhances message fluency, thereby encouraging consumers to make more environmentally friendly decisions. Sundar and Kellaris (2015) noted that both green and blue packaging evoke similar environmental judgments, as both colors are interpreted as eco-friendly.

A further theoretical contribution of this research lies in its examination of the role of textual information on eco-label logos and its influence on consumers' perceptions of sustainability, label credibility, and label usage. While previous studies have shown that visual elements—such as logos and images—are often more effective in enhancing consumer recall and recognition (Kaplan et al., 1968), this study highlights the importance of textual components in shaping perceptions of eco-labels and, more broadly, sustainable goods. This finding aligns with the results of Donato and D'Aniello (2022), who indicate that textual informational cues on eco-labels significantly enhance consumers' perceptions of food quality, sustainability, and ethicality. Finally, the limited recognition of eco-labels reported by study participants aligns with findings from previous research in the eco-label domain, highlighting low consumer awareness of these green signals (e.g., Donato & D'Aniello, 2022; Eldesouky et al., 2020; Grunert et al., 2014; Meyerding & Merz, 2018; Song et al., 2019).

3　IMPLICATIONS FOR PRACTITIONERS AND POLICYMAKERS

Professionals seeking to leverage eco-labels will find valuable insights in the systematic literature review, which provides a comprehensive overview of the various types, benefits, and mechanisms of eco-labels, along with successful business case studies. This knowledge empowers marketers to integrate eco-labels into their strategies more effectively, fostering consumer trust and loyalty. Furthermore, the analysis of aesthetic dimensions in consumer perceptions reveals how visual design impacts marketing effectiveness, offering actionable insights for creating more compelling and persuasive materials. Finally, the empirical findings in Chapter 4 offer practical guidance for refining eco-label strategies to drive sustainable purchasing decisions.

One of the key findings of the abovementioned empirical study is that visual complexity can enhance consumer perceptions of sustainability. For managers, this suggests that investing in more intricate and visually sophisticated eco-label designs can help signal environmental care and commitment. However, this complexity must be carefully managed to avoid overwhelming consumers with overly complicated or ambiguous designs. In fact, results also show that conceptual clarity is essential for ensuring that consumers understand the label's message and trust its sustainability claims.

Green and blue backgrounds were found to significantly enhance perceived sustainability, suggesting that companies should leverage these colors when designing eco-labels for products with strong environmental credentials. However, it is crucial to ensure that the use of these colors is backed by genuine sustainability practices to avoid accusations of greenwashing.

The study also found that textual information on eco-labels positively influences consumer perceptions of sustainability and drives adoption. Consumers are more likely to trust and adopt eco-labeled products when the labels provide detailed, transparent information about the product's environmental benefits. This aligns with broader trends in consumer demand for transparency, particularly in markets where sustainability is a credence attribute—one that cannot be easily verified by the consumer without access to detailed information.

Managers should ensure that eco-labels include clear and concise information about the specific environmental attributes of the product, such as whether it is organic, fair trade, or made from recycled materials. This not only builds consumer trust but also provides a basis for differentiation in competitive markets where many products claim to be sustainable. Moreover, companies can use digital tools such as QR codes to provide additional layers of information, allowing consumers to engage more deeply with the product's sustainability credentials.

Another critical finding from the research is the role of label recognition in influencing both perceived sustainability and adoption. Consumers are more likely to trust and adopt eco-labeled products when they are familiar with the label.

For managers, this means that investments in awareness campaigns are crucial to building consumer recognition of eco-labels. Companies can partner with established certification bodies to co-brand their products with widely recognized eco-labels, thereby leveraging existing trust and familiarity. Additionally, companies can use social media, influencer marketing, and educational content to raise awareness of lesser-known eco-labels, building familiarity and trust over time.

The research also highlights the importance of considering demographic and psychographic factors in eco-label adoption. Age, environmental concern, and label recognition all play significant roles in shaping consumer responses to eco-labels. For example, older consumers were found to be more skeptical of eco-labels, while those with higher environmental consciousness were more likely to perceive eco-labeled products as sustainable.

The results are particularly relevant for designers, who should incorporate intricate visual elements that catch consumers' eyes while ensuring that the core message remains easily understandable. This balance is crucial, as previous research indicates that overly complex designs can increase cognitive load and lead to negative evaluations (Miceli et al., 2014). Designers must refine their approaches to label aesthetics by focusing on clear symbolism and straightforward messaging that resonate with consumers.

Strategic use of color is another critical consideration. The study suggests that green and blue backgrounds are effective in evoking sustainability perceptions. Designers should leverage these colors to enhance aesthetic appeal and reinforce environmental messages. Additionally, textual information should complement visual elements without overwhelming them. By thoughtfully integrating text that clearly communicates the eco-label's purpose, designers can create labels that attract attention while providing consumers with the necessary information to make informed purchasing decisions. Moreover, designers should collaborate with marketing teams to ensure that eco-labels are not only aesthetically pleasing but also supported by robust advertising strategies. Incorporating textual elements that explain the label's meaning will help reinforce the eco-label's message when promoted through social media and other advertising avenues. This synergy between design and marketing will maximize consumer engagement and comprehension.

Retailers also play a vital role in the visibility and effectiveness of eco-labels. According to the findings, retailers should prioritize stocking products featuring well-designed eco-labels that incorporate intricate designs and appropriate color schemes. Additionally, the presence of private labels increasingly matched with eco-labels presents a unique opportunity for retailers. When choosing specific eco-labels, those that align with the present findings should be prioritized for selection and highlighted in marketing efforts.

Retailers can implement strategic marketing campaigns that showcase these eco-labeled products through in-store displays, promotional materials, and advertisements on their websites and social media platforms. Highlighting eco-labels in-store flyers can further enhance consumer awareness and interest. Training sales staff to effectively articulate the benefits of eco-labels will also improve customer engagement. By promoting products with high-quality eco-labels and ensuring that private labels are aligned with sustainable practices, retailers can cater to the growing market of environmentally conscious consumers, thereby driving sales and fostering brand loyalty.

Policymakers can also derive valuable insights from this book regarding the promotion of sustainable consumption and the enhancement of the regulatory framework for eco-labels. The findings underscore the need for clearer standards and guidelines for eco-label usage, as many consumers find it challenging to interpret their meanings, which undermines their effectiveness in promoting sustainability. Collaboration between policymakers, certification bodies, and industry stakeholders is essential to develop standardized, easily understood eco-labels that consumers can readily recognize and trust.

Additionally, policymakers could implement regulations that govern both the criteria for eco-label certifications and their visual design. This would ensure that labels are not only informative—incorporating textual information, visual elements directly associated with sustainability, and colors typically linked to eco-friendliness, such as green or blue—but also feature engaging visual designs characterized by high visual complexity. This initiative could enhance consumer confidence in eco-labeled products and foster broader adoption of sustainable practices.

Moreover, governments and regulatory bodies should invest in public awareness campaigns to educate consumers about the significance of eco-labels. As sustainability becomes increasingly urgent, it is vital for consumers to be equipped with the knowledge necessary for informed purchasing decisions. These campaigns could focus on increasing the visibility of eco-labels and clarifying the environmental and social criteria they represent.

Furthermore, policymakers should promote consumer education initiatives through advertising campaigns. Collaborating with industry stakeholders to create informative content that elucidates the significance of eco-labels can enhance overall consumer awareness. Utilizing social media platforms for these educational initiatives can effectively reach a wider audience and engage younger consumers. By supporting robust advertising and educational efforts, policymakers can drive the adoption of sustainable products and contribute to a more environmentally conscious marketplace.

4   Limitations and Future Research Directions

While this book has provided a comprehensive overview of the literature on eco-labels and aesthetics in consumer behavior, the systematic literature reviews revealed some limitations that warrant further exploration in future research. Firstly, the predominant focus on consumer research may have constrained the understanding of eco-labels and aesthetic dimensions. Future studies could benefit from incorporating interdisciplinary approaches, drawing insights from fields such as psychology, design, and environmental studies. Additionally, the emergence of new aesthetic trends stemming from social media and web platforms has not been addressed. Investigating how these trends influence consumer perceptions could provide valuable insights for both researchers and practitioners in the evolving landscape of sustainability communication.

More importantly, the empirical study illustrated in Chapter 4 opens several avenues for future research. First, while the focus was on fifteen real-world eco-labels, which allowed the exploration of consumer evaluations in a naturalistic setting, the use of fictional eco-labels might have eliminated familiarity or exposure effects. Future studies could address this by incorporating fictitious eco-labels to enable controlled manipulation of graphical dimensions, thereby isolating cause-effect relationships more effectively. An experimental study manipulating these visual variables could be conducted to confirm the results found in this research.

Additionally, although the fifteen selected eco-labels cover a broad range of sustainability types, the findings could be influenced by the vast diversity of eco-labels currently available. According to the Ecolabel

Index, the marketplace includes a vast array of eco-labels, indicating that further research should evaluate a more extensive set of labels to enhance the generalizability of the conclusions. Nonetheless, the graphical diversity within the studied eco-labels—specifically the variations in visual and conceptual complexity, text amount, and color—provides a strong foundation for future investigations into how eco-label design impacts sustainability perceptions.

The present research focuses solely on the design of Type I eco-labels, which primarily utilize visual elements and colors associated with sustainability, without considering Type II and Type III eco-labels. Future research could expand the analysis to include Type II and Type III eco-labels, exploring how their design elements and messaging strategies influence consumer perceptions and behaviors.

The study centered on consumer sustainability perceptions and label adoption, but future research could enhance these insights by incorporating behavioral data from real purchasing environments, and using tracking in marketplace settings to validate the results.

Moreover, the present research did not investigate the underlying mechanisms that explain the relationships between visual design and sustainability perceptions. Future studies should explore these mechanisms to gain a deeper understanding of how visual complexity, conceptual complexity, color background, and the amount of textual information impact consumers' sustainability perceptions. Additionally, it would be valuable to assess whether these findings remain consistent when multiple eco-labels are tested across various exposure settings.

Furthermore, the study concentrated on a limited range of background colors (green, blue, white, and black), which are commonly associated with sustainability. However, future research should expand the color spectrum to include other tones, such as brown, which may evoke different sustainability perceptions (e.g., Donato et al., 2021). Understanding how a broader range of colors influences consumer preferences could provide deeper insights into eco-label design.

The study also confirmed a positive relationship between visual complexity and the dependent variables (e.g., sustainability perceptions and label use). However, the effects of conceptual complexity were affected by eco-label familiarity, indicating that repeated exposure to eco-labels might shape how conceptual elements are interpreted. Future research should investigate the role of repeated exposure in identifying the optimal balance between visual complexity and conceptual clarity, ensuring that eco-labels are engaging and easy to understand over time.

Furthermore, the study focused specifically on four key graphical elements—visual complexity, conceptual complexity, color, and text—limiting the scope of variables examined. Additional collative and psychographic factors, such as symmetry, size, and novelty, could influence eco-label perceptions and should be included in future research for a more comprehensive understanding of eco-label effectiveness.

Lastly, the sample for this study consisted of young Italian consumers, which may limit the generalizability of the findings to other age groups and cultural contexts. Consumer responses to eco-labels could differ across cultures due to variations in design interpretation, sustainability priorities, and eco-label familiarity. Future research should broaden the scope by considering cross-cultural studies and a wider age range to explore whether the observed relationships between visual complexity, conceptual complexity, and sustainability perceptions hold across different demographic segments.

The issue of greenwashing, where eco-labels are used to signal environmental responsibility without meaningful commitments, also remains an important area for future research. As companies increasingly adopt eco-labels in their marketing strategies, it is essential to explore how consumers perceive eco-labels' credibility and transparency. Future studies could examine the interaction between visual and conceptual complexity and greenwashing perceptions to develop design strategies that enhance consumer trust.

Additionally, the role of emerging technologies, such as augmented reality (AR) and virtual reality (VR), in enhancing the visual impact of eco-labels presents an exciting avenue for further exploration. As AR and VR become more integrated into marketing and retail experiences, researchers could explore how these technologies influence consumer perceptions of sustainability and eco-label aesthetics.

REFERENCES

Atkinson, L., & Rosenthal, S. (2014). Signaling the green sell: The influence of eco-label source, argument specificity, and product involvement on consumer trust. *Journal of Advertising, 43*(1), 33–45.

Berlyne, D. E. (1970). Novelty, complexity, and hedonic value. *Perception & Psychophysics, 8*(5), 279–286.

Bickart, B. A., & Ruth, J. A. (2012). Green eco-seals and advertising persuasion. *Journal of Advertising, 41*(4), 51–67.

Bloch, P. H. (1995). Seeking the ideal form: Product design and consumer response. *Journal of Marketing, 59*(3), 16–29.

Bornstein, R. F. (1989). Exposure and affect: Overview and meta-analysis of research, 1968–1987. *Psychological Bulletin, 106*(2), 265.

Creusen, M. E., & Schoormans, J. P. (2005). The different roles of product appearance in consumer choice. *Journal of Product Innovation Management, 22*(1), 63–81.

Dekhili, S., & Achabou, M. A. (2014). Eco-labelling brand strategy: Independent certification versus self-declaration. *European Business Review, 26*(4), 305–329.

Donato, C., & Adıgüzel, F. (2022). Visual complexity of eco-labels and product evaluations in online setting: Is simple always better? *Journal of Retailing and Consumer Services, 67*, 102961.

Donato, C., & Adıgüzel, F. (2024). The effects of visual design on eco-labels evaluations: Guidelines for effective green advertising. *Journal of Marketing Theory and Practice*, 1–18.

Donato, C., & D'Aniello, A. (2022). Tell me more and make me feel proud: The role of eco-labels and informational cues on consumers' food perceptions. *British Food Journal, 124*(4).

Donato, C., Barone, A. M., & Romani, S. (2021). The satiating power of sustainability: The effect of package sustainability on perceived satiation of healthy food. *British Food Journal, 123*(13), 162–177.

Eldesouky, A., Mesias, F. J., & Escribano, M. (2020). Perception of Spanish consumers towards environmentally friendly labelling in food. *International Journal of Consumer Studies, 44*(1), 64–76.

Gaspar Ferreira, A., & Fernandes, M. E. (2022). Sustainable advertising or ecolabels: Which is the best for your brand and for consumers' environmental consciousness? *Journal of Marketing Theory and Practice, 30*(1), 20–36.

Grunert, K. G., Hieke, S., & Wills, J. (2014). Sustainability labels on food products: Consumer motivation, understanding and use. *Food Policy, 44*, 177–189.

Henderson, P. W., & Cote, J. A. (1998). Guidelines for selecting or modifying logos. *Journal of Marketing, 62*(2), 14–30.

Jiang, Y., Gorn, G. J., Galli, M., & Chattopadhyay, A. (2016). Does your company have the right logo? How and why circular-and angular-logo shapes influence brand attribute judgments. *Journal of Consumer Research, 42*(5), 709–726.

Kaplan, S., Kaplan, R., & Sampson, J. R. (1968). Encoding and arousal factors in free recall of verbal and visual material. *Psychonomic Science, 12*(2), 73–74.

Labrecque, L. I., & Milne, G. R. (2012). Exciting red and competent blue: The importance of color in marketing. *Journal of the Academy of Marketing Science, 40*(5), 711–727.

Labrecque, L. I., Patrick, V. M., & Milne, G. R. (2013). The marketers' prismatic palette: A review of color research and future directions. *Psychology & Marketing, 30*(2), 187–202.

Lim, D., Baek, T. H., Yoon, S., & Kim, Y. (2020). Colour effects in green advertising. *International Journal of Consumer Studies, 44*(6), 552–562.

Mai, R., Symmank, C., & Seeberg-Elverfeldt, B. (2016). Light and pale colors in food packaging: When does this package cue signal superior healthiness or inferior tastiness? *Journal of Retailing, 92*(4), 426–444.

Majer, J. M., Henscher, H. A., Reuber, P., Fischer-Kreer, D., & Fischer, D. (2022). The effects of visual sustainability labels on consumer perception and behavior: A systematic review of the empirical literature. *Sustainable Production and Consumption, 33*, 1–14.

Meyerding, S. G., & Merz, N. (2018). Consumer preferences for organic labels in Germany using the example of apples–combining choice-based conjoint analysis and eye-tracking measurements. *Journal of Cleaner Production, 181*, 772–783.

Miceli, G. N., Scopelliti, I., Raimondo, M. A., & Donato, C. (2014). Breaking through complexity: Visual and conceptual dimensions in logo evaluation across exposures. *Psychology & Marketing, 31*(10), 886–899.

Nickel, K., & Böhm, R. A. (2024). Power versus morality: Uncovering the underlying mechanisms of consumer response to perceived visual sustainability in package design. *Journal of Product & Brand Management.*

Seo, J. Y., & Scammon, D. L. (2017). Do green packages lead to misperceptions? The influence of package colours on consumers' perceptions of brands with environmental claims. *Marketing Letters, 28*(3), 357–369.

Sigurdsson, V., Larsen, N. M., Pálsdóttir, R. G., Folwarczny, M., Menon, R. V., & Fagerstrøm, A. (2022). Increasing the effectiveness of ecological food signaling: Comparing sustainability tags with eco-labels. *Journal of Business Research, 139*, 1099–1110.

Sirieix, L., Delanchy, M., Remaud, H., Zepeda, L., & Gurviez, P. (2013). Consumers' perceptions of individual and combined sustainable food labels: A UK pilot investigation. *International Journal of Consumer Studies, 37*(2), 143–151.

Song, L., Lim, Y., Chang, P., Guo, Y., Zhang, M., Wang, X., ... & Cai, H. (2019). Ecolabel's role in informing sustainable consumption: A naturalistic decision making study using eye tracking glasses. *Journal of cleaner production, 218*, 685–695.

Sundar, A., & Kellaris, J. J. (2015). Blue-washing the green halo: How colors color ethical judgments. In *The psychology of design* (pp. 63–74). Routledge.

Sundar, A., & Kellaris, J. J. (2017). How logo colors influence shoppers' judgments of retailer ethicality: The mediating role of perceived eco-friendliness. *Journal of Business Ethics, 146,* 685–701.

Tang, E., Fryxell, G. E., & Chow, C. S. (2004). Visual and verbal communication in the design of eco-label for green consumer products. *Journal of International Consumer Marketing, 16*(4), 85–105.

Teisl, M. F., Peavey, S., Newman, F., Buono, J., & Hermann, M. (2002). Consumer reactions to environmental labels for forest products: A preliminary look. *Forest Products Journal, 52*(1), 44.

Teisl, M. F., Rubin, J., & Noblet, C. L. (2008). Non-dirty dancing? Interactions between eco-labels and consumers. *Journal of Economic Psychology, 29*(2), 140–159.

Thøgersen, J. (2000). Psychological determinants of paying attention to eco-labels in purchase decisions: Model development and multinational validation. *Journal of Consumer Policy, 23*(3), 285–313.

Veryzer, R. W., Jr., & Hutchinson, J. W. (1998). The influence of unity and prototypicality on aesthetic responses to new product designs. *Journal of Consumer Research, 24*(4), 374–394.

Wang, X., Chen, J., Ma, C., & Jiang, Y. (2024) Simpler is greener: The impact of packaging visual complexity on products' eco-friendliness perception. *Psychology & Marketing.*

Zajonc, R. B. (1968). Attitudinal effects of mere exposure. *Journal of Personality and Social Psychology, 9*(2p2), 1.

Index

© The Editor(s) (if applicable) and The Author(s), under exclusive
license to Springer Nature Switzerland AG 2025
C. Donato, *Eco-Label Visual Design and Sustainability*,
https://doi.org/10.1007/978-3-031-82761-7

The manufacturer's authorised representative in the EU is Springer
Nature Customer Service Centre GmbH, Europaplatz 3, 69115 Heidelberg,
Germany. If you have any concerns regarding our products, please
contact ProductSafety@springernature.com

Printed and bound by CPI Group (UK) Ltd, Croydon, CR0 4YY

24/04/2026

02096368-0001